IRREGARDLESS...
ain't a word.

1st ~~Addition~~
Edition

Chip and Chazz:
Learning from their mistakes

(~~Buy too~~ guys, John Schwietz and Patrick ~~Hawkin's~~)
By two   *Hawkins*

P.O. Box 743 Willernie, MN 55090-0743
Library of Congress Cataloging-in-Publication Data
ISBN: 978-0-615-54605-6

First Printing
Please visit:
irregardlessbook.com

Dedicated to "our baker's dozen."

Mom and Dad

Jack, Ben, Riley and Becki

Elizabeth, Katherine, Rebecca and Kristine

Ava, Cole and Jennifer

ForewOrd (note: Not "Forward" or "Foreward")
A note to parents and educators.

The way we communicate is changing. It is changing constantly.

Do you remember when you would write a letter to someone, fold it and put it in an envelope? Lick a stamp, stick it on the envelope, look up the address of the person to whom you are writing in the phone book (or in your address book), place the letter in your mailbox, flip up the flag on the mailbox and wait for a response… in a week or two? It seems like ancient history.

The careful letter writer would likely have a copy of their favorite dictionary available for reference… just to be "sure".

You were your own "word processor." You were your own "spell check."

Sending a letter to someone has become rare. Handwriting a letter is virtually unheard of.

Today, we pull out our smart phone, compose a text message or tweet as expeditiously as possible, hit "send text" and wait for a response… in a minute or two.

What will tomorrow bring?

Obviously, modern communication technology has allowed us to become more accomplished. Today, we communicate with more people much faster.

Is today's communication better? Maybe. Maybe not.

It is faster. It has allowed us to efficiently communicate to significantly more people.

Unfortunately, the message you might be communicating is "I am a careless writer." You are sending that message. You are sending that message much faster and to significantly more people.

The fact is that many people are not concerned with details of carefully crafted, accurate communication; but many people are. People who make decisions about things like hiring employees are concerned about this good communication. A simple mistake can mean the difference between being hired for a job or being passed over. Modern communication technology undermines proper, intelligent communication in many ways.

This book may not make you a better person. *Irregardless* is intended to help you become a more thoughtful communicator, a better writer and a more intelligent sounding speaker. In some ways, this book is simply intended to help you expand and refine your vocabulary. In some ways, it is simply to make you aware of potential pitfalls. On second thought, perhaps this book *will* make you a better person.

Many of the issues addressed herein are very simple, obvious mistakes people make. Unfortunately, they are common and becoming more common.

The goal of *IRREGARDLESS* is to change the way people think about communicating 360 degrees (just checking if you are still reading... we meant 180 degrees). Communicate thoughtfully. Communicate carefully. *IRREGARDLESS* will help you build a better vocabulary.

there   too   lessons

Hopefully, ~~their~~ are just ~~to~~ many ~~lessens~~ presented in this book for you to ignore. The desire to improve should help ~~peek~~ your interest in *Irregardless*.

pique

Most importantly, *Irregardless* is fun. The way the story and lessons are presented is unlike anything you have ever seen.

CONTENTS

Meet our Heroes: Introducing Chip and Chazz

CHIP PHILLIPPO

Given name: Donald Irving Phillippo

24 years old / 5'11" 230 lbs. ("Big Guy")

College Graduate

Four-year degree in four years

Unsuccessful Realtor

Regular Guy

Likeable

Friendly

CHAZZ SEVERSON

Given name: Charles Ernest Severson

26 years old / 6'1" 190 lbs.

College Graduate

Four-year degree in six years

Car Salesman

Aspiring "motivational speaker"

Strikingly Handsome (just ask him…)

Meet our Heroine:* Introducing Sister Scholastica Bailey (1916-2009)

Sister Scholastica was Principal of Grace Junior High School from 1966-1996. She was trained as an English teacher. She became famous for her often used *red pen (look forward to seeing this)*.

Sister Scholastica passed away in 2009 at the age of 93. She's gone... but not really. Her memory lives on in all of her friends.

Her *lessons* "live" on in many of her students... just not Chip and Chazz.

The spirit of Sister Scholastica continues to look down upon her friends, family and her students. Chip and Chazz, however, occupy an inordinate amount of Sister Scholastica's energy.

What a difference a single letter can make

Heroine:

1.   A woman of distinguished courage or ability, admired for her brave deeds and noble qualities.
2.   The principal female character in a story

Heroin:

1.   A white, crystalline, narcotic powder, $C_{21}H_{23}NO_5$, derived from morphine, formerly used as an analgesic and sedative. Manufacture and importation of heroin are now controlled by federal law in the U.S. because of the danger of addiction.

Chapter 1

Meet Chip

Today was the day. It just had to be. Exactly ten weeks ago, Chip Phillippo had spent an entire Saturday in a stuffy classroom at Century College in the St. Paul suburb of White Bear Lake, Minnesota.

He was there on a late October day to take the Federal Civil Service Exam. Jobs were scarce. Only the United States Government seemed to be hiring, so Chip figured he should "play the odds."

The government official charged with administering the exam told the 40 hopeful candidates, "Expect to receive your exam results in the mail sometime in the next 8-10 weeks."

Two weeks ago, at exactly the eight-week mark, Chip began his daily routine of waiting outside his parents' home for the daily U.S. mail.

Chip had become acquainted with the mail carrier who had been delivering mail to his family home for nearly 15 years. They had become friends.

Chip could see the mail truck working its way down his block. It seemed to be moving slower than usual. "What is taking so long?" Chip anxiously asked himself.

Chip nonchalantly strolled toward the approaching mail truck. There was nothing nonchalant about how he felt.

"Good morning, Mr. Tufte," Chip greeted the friendly mailman as he had done occasionally for the past 15 years and every day for the past two weeks.

"Good morning, Donald." The chubby mail carrier had known Chip by his real name (from Chip's *Boy's Life* subscription) long before Donald became known as "Chip."

The origin of Chip's nickname is unclear. Chip liked to think it was because of his self-described "superior short game in golf." Most of his friends remember the name coming from his superior interest in potato chips.

"Anything interesting in the mail today?" Chip asked with a hint of nervousness in his voice.

Mr. Tufte knew what Chip was waiting for. Chip had been keeping his mail carrier friend apprised of the situation, hopeful that the postman would somehow expedite the delivery of his special letter.

"I think you might be interested in today's bundle," Tufte joked. "I know you have been waiting for the latest Pottery Barn catalog." The joke seemed to work. Chip laughed momentarily and quickly reverted back to his anxious posture, "No, seriously… anything good?"

The mail on this particular day included a handful of catalogs, holiday greetings from local insurance agents and a couple of envelopes.

It was the envelopes that caught Chip's attention.

"Is there anything official?" Chip muttered to himself, turning his back on Mr. Tufte without saying a word. The kind mailman smiled to himself, understanding how important the mail can often be to his customers.

"I sure hope it's something good," Tufte whispered to himself as he drove off to the next cluster of mailboxes.

Chapter 2

Meet Chazz

Just northeast of St. Paul in Mahtomedi, Minnesota, Charles Ernest Severson was also waiting for the mail.

Chazz, as he was known, was waiting for his latest issue of *Ab Fitness* and *Sports International.* He had been out late the night before. He was out late most nights. Since college, Chazz considered his night-life an important networking opportunity. At least, that is what he told his parents (or his neighbors, as he called them).

His parents had converted the space above their garage into a very nice efficiency apartment for their only son. Chazz had convinced himself that this apartment qualified as a separate residence because he had a separate entrance. The separate entrance was actually a converted fire escape originally built to satisfy a city building code requirement.

After moving out of his parents' home, Chazz placed his own mailbox right next to his parents'. The mailbox was a nice cedar box he had built in his woodworking class in high school. He got an "A" on the project and it had sat on his bedroom dresser like a trophy.

The weathered grade sheet had still been attached to the mailbox until he decided to use it for mail at his new place. He removed the grade sheet and carefully placed it into a scrapbook his mother had made for him when he graduated from high school.

While the mail carrier was under no obligation to separate the daily mail, Chazz bribed him with Minnesota Wild hockey tickets to place *his* mail into *his* mailbox.

Chazz and Chip have been best friends since the 7th grade. They met at Grace Junior High School (Chip's first attempt at 7th grade and the *second* for Chazz).

Unlike Chip, there is no question about the origin of Charles' nickname; he gave it to himself. He started introducing himself as "Chazz" while in seventh grade. It just felt right.

"*Ab Fitness* has an awesome article on sculpting abs," Chazz told his mail carrier, Jay. Jay really didn't care.

Jay removed the *Chazz-mail* from his parents' and sarcastically said, "Here you go Mr. Fitness." Chazz didn't notice the sarcasm.

The 26 year-old Chazz had an unusual amount of mail today. His Abs magazine was there and that was all he really cared about. Physical appearance was unusually important to Chazz.

He did not notice the letter from the United States Federal Testing Authority.

His civil service exam results were in and Chazz couldn't care less. He had crunches and sit-ups to do. At that moment, Chazz was only interested in his abs. He also needed to email his friend Chip about his night of networking the previous night.

Chazz also failed to notice the small white envelope among the mail. No return address, only his name and address.

It was a letter that would change the direction of his life forever and he pitched it aside as he did with the coupons for the neighborhood grocery store which he never used. He didn't need them, because he ate dinner at his neighbors' home every night.

Subject: ~~Your~~ never going to guess who I ~~seen~~ yesterday
You're   *saw*
Sent by: Charles Severson (Chazz)
On: January 02 10:08 AM
To: Chip Phillippo
Reply to: Chazz

What up Chipster,

there

Great party last night. I was hoping to see you ~~their~~. Check it out,
I was sitting at the bar and I looked across the room and saw that
brainiac Preston Gorg.

Do you remember Preston? He was the kid who gave that speech
at graduation from high school. I am not sure why they picked that
goof to give that lame speech. Remember, he went on and on about
our future and all the great things that we have to look forward to.

You have to call me. He is like a billionaire and has this unbelievably
cute girlfriend, some gal he met at grad school. He invented
something that helps people with some kind of disease or something.
He is still a goof ball, just a rich goof ball. He said he was interested
in buying a new car. I plan to email him later today.

Regardless
~~Irregardless~~ of how rich he is or how awesome his girlfriend is, that
dude is still a bit of a nerd. I will, however, be happy to sell that nerd
a new car!

Call me. I guess that nerds really do rule the world.

Lesson A

- **Your and You're-**

    "Your"- pronoun (a form of the possessive case of "you" used as an attributive adjective): For example, "Your pants look too tight."

    "You're"- contraction of "you are." For example, "You're certain you want to wear those pants?"

- **Seen and Saw-**

    "Seen"- is the past participle form of "see." Seen requires a "helper verb," such as "have." I have seen the nerd. A nerd was seen at the car dealership yesterday.

    "Saw"- is the past tense form of "see." "Saw" can be used by itself, without a helping verb. For example, you saw me. I saw the nerd. Don't ever use a helper verb with "saw." Could have saw. Should have saw. Wrong! "Could have seen" or "should have seen" is correct.

- **There, Their and They're-(one of the most common mistakes)**

    "There"- can be an adverb, pronoun, noun, adjective or interjection

    Adverb: in or at that place (opposed to here): Chip is there.

    Pronoun: That place: Chip went there, too.

    Noun: That state or condition: You're on your own from there on.

    Adjective: Used for emphasis: Check out that nerd there.

    Interjection: (used to express satisfaction): There! I'm done.

    "Their"- can only be used as a pronoun: Their monkey was wearing pants.

    Pronoun: a form of the possessive case of "they" used as an attributive.

    "They're"- is a contraction of "they are"

- **Irregardless-** *DON'T USE IT!* The word to use is *regardless.*

    "Irregardless" is considered "nonstandard" because of the two negative elements ir- and -less. A bad combination of *irrespective* (which is a word) and *regardless* (which is also a word).

Chapter 3

DIP

Just as he had hoped, today was the day. Chip had been anxiously waiting for this moment for exactly ten weeks. There were two envelopes in his mail. One was from the United States Testing Authority (USTA). It was just as Chip had imagined, very official looking.

The other was a simple white envelope, with no return address, just Chip's name, address and a postage stamp; probably a bill or something.

Chip brought the mail into his home and tossed the catalogs into a basket with dozens of other unread items. The rest of the mail was placed on the corner of his kitchen table.

The only item that mattered was the letter from the USTA. "Should I just rip it open?" he whispered. "You're talking to yourself again!" he sarcastically reminded himself.

He took out the pewter letter-opener that his Aunt Barbi bought for him upon his graduation from the University of Minnesota. It had the University's "M" on one side of the handle and his initials "DIP" on the other side. (His parents failed to recognize the issues that would come with using Chip's maternal grandfather's name "Irving" as Chip's middle name. As a result, Chip will likely never own monogrammed shirts.)

Chip placed the blade of his fancy opener into the corner of the envelope and carefully sliced it open. He removed the letter and set the folded one-page document on the table in front of him.

"One page?" he was nervously talking to himself again. "That can't be good, can it?"

He unfolded the letter and read…

Dear Mr. Phillippo,

Thank you for taking the Federal Civil Service Exam (FCSE). The United States depends upon the patriotism and talent of its citizens. The success of our country requires the dedicated service of talented people like you.

Your scores were excellent. We appreciate your interest in working for the United States. We hope you found the process satisfactory.

Warm Regards,

FCSE Administration

"THAT'S IT?" he shouted at the letter. He flipped it over to see if there was anything written on the back. "A STINKING FORM LETTER IS ALL I GET? MY SCORES WERE EXCELLENT!" his voice cracked as he tore open the envelope hoping he had missed something. There was nothing.

He sulked to the kitchen cupboard and grabbed an open bag of potato chips. Chip often found comfort in salty snacks. Today would be no exception.

He sat back down and recklessly ripped open the rest of the mail. As usual, there was nothing but a bunch of marketing junk.

He finally came to the plain envelope. He tore it open and quickly read the one paragraph letter. His demeanor changed from anger to curiosity. In one minute, Chip had forgotten about the first letter he opened.

"What the heck is this?" he thought to himself, intrigued, but confused nonetheless.

Lesson B

	You're *saw*
Subject:	~~Your~~ never going to guess who I ~~seen~~ yesterday
Sent by:	Chip Phillippo
On:	January 02 10:18 AM
To:	Charles Severson (Chazz)
Reply to:	Chip

Hey Chazz,

Sounds like you had an interesting night. I wish I would have gone
to that party ~~to~~.
        too

I remember Preston. He wasn't such a bad guy. By the way, he was
valedictorian. He was the top student in our class.
               Principal
I could never understand why our ~~Principle~~, Sister Scholastica, was
so nice to you. You made fun of everyone, your grades were terrible
(even though you cheated constantly) and you were late to every
class... every day. It must have been your charming personality
that fooled her.
              passed
You know what? I kind of miss her since she ~~past~~ away. I wish
I could find a job with a boss like Sister.

Did you get anything interesting in the mail today?
Let me know.

I'll call you later. Maybe we can do something tonight. Are
you having dinner with your neighbors? ☺

Lesson B

- To, Too and Two-

  "To"- is most often a preposition. (used for expressing motion or direction toward a point, person, place, or thing approached and reached, as opposed to from): They came to the house.

  "Too"- is always an adverb

  1. In addition; also; furthermore; moreover: big, fat and stupid too.

  2. To an excessive extent or degree; too slow to win.

  3. More, as specified, than should be: too near the fire.

  4. Used as an affirmative to contradict a negative statement: Chip is too!

  5. Extremely; very: Chazz wasn't too pleased with his haircut.

  "Two" is the number 2.

- Principal and Principle-

  "Principal"- noun

  1. A chief or head.

  2. The head or director of a school or, esp. in England, a college.

  3. A person who takes a leading part in any activity, as a play; chief actor or doer.

  "Principle"- noun

  1. An accepted or professed rule of action or conduct: a person of good moral principles.

  2. A fundamental, primary, or general law or truth from which others are derived: the principles of proper grammar.

- Past and Passed-

  There is a difference. Be careful.

  "Past"- can be used as an adjective, adverb, noun or a preposition.

  "Passed"- is the past tense of the verb "to pass."

Chapter 4

Burger Barn?

What could *this* letter mean?

December 31   CONFIDENTIAL

Dear Donald Phillippo,

Your name was recently brought to our attention as a result of some testing that you participated in several months ago. After careful analysis of the exam results, representatives from our organization would like to visit with you to learn more about you and your interests. We would like to visit with you on January 7th at 7:00 A.M. at our local field office. We are located at 2525 University Avenue in St. Paul (The address provided is **not** a typo.)

Please come in and find a seat. We will come to you.

Please keep the details of this correspondence confidential.

Yours Truly,

Mr. Wright, CSA Regional Director

Cc: Neetenbeek

Mr. Wright? It sounds like it is made up. Who or what is a Neetenbeek? Why do I have to keep this confidential? Should I even go to this meeting? What could CSA stand for? How many people can I tell and still have it confidential?

Mr. Wright? I hope this isn't some kind of dating service.

Chip went to his laptop and did a search for "CSA". Could it stand for Comprehensive Salvage Association; Cincinnati Soccer Alliance; Confederate States of America; Confederate States of America? That sounds like a possibility. What could it be?

Chip thought to himself, with my luck, CSA could mean Creative Sandwich Association. Who knows?

He decided to get into his car and drive to 2525 University Avenue and see what the office building looked like. Maybe ask a few questions. He wanted to ask Chazz or his dad to go with him, but it said "confidential."

Chip made his way down Interstate 94 and took the exit near the Minnesota State Capitol Building. His anxiety about the situation grew the closer he got to University Avenue.

He drove to the area with all of the office buildings and was surprised that they ended at the 2100 block of University. The next several blocks were retail stores and restaurants. What could 2525 be?

He traveled past 2501 University Avenue. There it was, 2525 University Avenue. Big gold numbers 2525 above the front door. He looked again at the letter to make sure he had the right numbers.

He was definitely at the right address. 2525 University Avenue was a Burger Barn; a big one with a HUGE indoor playground.

Under normal circumstances, Chip would enjoy an invitation to dine at "the Barn". He liked Burger Barn, but this was a disappointment.

Chip thought to himself, "CSA? Creative Sandwich Agency? I just knew it! What could be confidential about Burger Barn? Maybe something to do with that special sauce. Perhaps it was the Confidential Sauce Association?"

Chapter 5

Nerds Rule

It was Monday morning. Chazz had to go to work. His dad helped him get a job selling used cars at Wally Melander's Cadillac dealership in the St. Paul suburb of Roseville. His dad had been friends with Wally for many years.

One of the reasons that Chazz loved the job, was because Wally would often let him drive one of the demos on the weekends. Chazz considered it smart marketing. At least that is what he told Wally. Wally considered it charity.

Wally was a very kind man. Despite some of Chazz's obvious character flaws, Wally liked Chazz and enjoyed the stories he would tell about the previous night's "networking." If there was one thing that Chazz Severson was good at, it was networking.

Chazz had been networking over the weekend at the St. Paul Grill. "The Grill," as he called it, was inside the St. Paul Hotel. Built in 1910, the St. Paul Hotel was the most elegant and historic hotel in Minnesota.

He had been dining at the St. Paul Grill with his sister and his parents for as long as he could remember. Anytime there was a special occasion, they went to The Grill.

He really liked it there. The restaurant General Manager and the entire staff knew Chazz and treated him well. His dad was always very generous in the "tipping" department. His years of generosity paid off for Chazz.

When Chazz wanted to impress a girl, he would take her to The Grill.

Chazz ran into some old high school friends on New Year's Eve. He was hoping that his classmate Preston Gorg would be stopping by the dealership to take a look at a new car. It was a new year and it would be awesome to start the year off with a big sale. Unfortunately for Chazz, Minnesota was experiencing another strong blizzard. They had 8 inches of snow and were expecting another 6 -10.

The ambitious young salesman had also become accustomed to people saying that they were planning to come to the dealership and then never showing up. Selling cars was tough. Chazz had become fairly good at handling rejection; it was just part of the job.

Not many customers ventured out in the snow on this particularly cold January morning. There was very little traffic at all. Chazz was about to pack up his things, when he heard his name paged over the sales floor intercom.

"Chazz Severson, guests waiting in the showroom. Chazz Severson please call the operator."

He was shocked. No one had ever come in and asked specifically for him. His sales had all come from patrolling the showroom like a vulture circling his prey.

Chazz quickly made his way out of the sales office, stopping quickly at the full-length mirror for one more glance. Everything looked good. He popped a mint into his mouth. Fresh breath was always a priority.

There he was, Preston Gorg and his gorgeous girlfriend peeking in the windows of a new Escalade. "Maybe he wasn't such a nerd," Chazz thought. He clearly has good taste in cars and better taste in girls.

Lesson C

Chazz:	"Greetings old friend."
Preston:	"Hello, Chazz (said a bit sarcastically), it is good to see you, too."
Chazz:	"Thanks for coming in… and who is this most lovely lady?"
	(Said with left eyebrow raised like a cheesy James Bond)
Preston:	"This is my fiancée*, Krisi Harmon, I think you met her (hit on her) Sunday night at the party."
Chazz:	"Oh, of course, so pleased to meet you."
Krisi:	"Hi Chazz, we've met." (said even more sarcastically)
Chazz:	"So Krisi, where did you meet my old friend, Preston?"
Krisi:	"We met at school."
Chazz:	"Oh, that means you must be quite smart; what do you do?"
Krisi:	"Chazz, I am a nuclear physicist."
Chazz:	"Nu-cu-ler physicist, very impressive Preston, not just another pretty face."
Krisi:	"Chazz, it is pronounced NU-CLEAR" (enunciated* slowly)
Chazz:	"Nu-CU-LER." (said slowly, staring confusedly at Krisi's lips)
Krisi:	"New-CLEEEEE-ERRRRR"
Chazz:	"Nu-CU-LER… (Chazz remebered that President George W. Bush pronounced it like he did. The President MUST be right.)
Krisi:	Frustrated, she said, "I am a physicist."
Chazz:	"Well Mr. and Mrs. Nu-Cu-Ler… what brings you in today?"
Preston:	"I am looking for something safe, maybe an SUV."
Chazz:	"I see that you have discovered the Escalade." (winking at Krisi) Were you looking to drive it off the lot today?
Preston:	"No, but I would like to have something new in time for the University Cancer Benefit in April. I have a bunch of guests coming to town and I need something big."
Chazz:	"I feel you. Tell me about the cancer benefit. I might be interested in helping out. I consider myself a bit of a philanthropist."
Krisi:	"I can totally see that Chazz." (said with a snicker)
Chazz:	"Thank you Krisi." (said with absolute sincerity)

Lesson C

- Fiancé and Fiancée-

    Fiancé- [fee-ahn-sey] –noun- a man engaged to be married; a man to whom a woman is engaged.

    Fiancée- [fee-ahn-sey]- noun- a woman engaged to be married; a woman to whom a man is engaged.

- Nuclear and "Nucular"- (pronunciation guide)

    [Noo-Cleer]-correct

    [Noo-cue-ler]-not correct... not a word

- Pronunciation- [noo-klee-er, nyoo- or, by metathesis*, -kyuh-ler]

    *metathesis: the transposition of letters, syllables, or sounds in a word, as in the pronunciation (in other words… "said the wrong way.")

Lesson D

Chazz: "Preston, I am not sure if you knew this but my Dad had ~~prostrate~~ cancer a couple of years ago."

prostate

Preston: "I am sorry to hear that. *Prostate* (with emphasis) cancer can be tough. Has he been treated?"

Chazz: "Yeah, he is doing much better. He underwent a strict ~~regiment~~. Diet, exercise and chemotherapy really helped!" *regimen*

Preston: "The medical community has made significant advances in cancer research and patient care."

Chazz: "Enough about him. Let's talk about getting you the car you want."

Preston: "I really like this new one, but I would love to get it in white."

Chazz: "White ones are tough to get, we are ~~supposably~~ getting a new shipment next week." *supposedly*

Krisi: "I bet you have people lined up around the block waiting for those white ones."

Chazz: "We do, but I have the inside track on a brand new pearl white coming in tomorrow."

Preston: "I'll take it."

Chazz: "Great. Preston, I have to be honest with you. I know that I wasn't always that nice to you in school. I appreciate your willingness to do business with me."

Preston: "No worries Chazz; it never really bothered me too much."

Chazz: "I am happy to know that the ~~statue~~ of limitations has run out on my bad behavior." *statute*

Preston: "By the way, do you ever see your old friend Chip?"

Chazz: "I see him all the time. He is a ~~relator~~ right now." *realtor*

Preston: "I always liked Chip."

Chazz: "He is looking for something new to do. He wants to work for the government. Enough about Chip, let's get this written up and get you and your lady back on the road."

Lesson D

• Prostate and Prostrate-

Prostate- noun (anatomy) - an organ that surrounds the urethra of males at the base of the bladder.

Prostrate- verb (used with object)

1. To cast (oneself) face down on the ground in humility.
2. To lay flat, as on the ground.

-Adjective

1. Lying flat or at full length, as on the ground.

• Regimen and Regiment*–

Regimen– noun- Medicine/Medical. A regulated course, as of diet, exercise, or manner of living, intended to preserve or restore health or to attain some result.

Regiment– when used as a noun- Military. A unit of ground forces, consisting of two or more battalions or battle groups, a headquarters unit and certain supporting units.

• Supposedly and "supposably" (not a word)

Pronunciation: [suh-**poh**-zid-lee] or, by metathesis*, -suh-**poh**-zub-lee]

*metathesis: the transposition of letters, syllables, or sounds in a word, as in the pronunciation (in other words… "said the wrong way.")

• Statute and Statue… very simple, the proper word is STATU<u>T</u>E, when used with "of limitations."

• Realtor and "Relator*"-

Pronunciation: [**reel**-tohr] -2 syllable word.

*metathesis: the transposition of letters, syllables, or sounds in a word, as in the pronunciation (in other words… "said the wrong way.")

Chapter 6

What are *you* doing here?

7:00 was very early on a Saturday morning. A 7:00 meeting meant Chip had to be out of bed no later than 5:30. He wondered if he had ever been up this early on a Saturday morning. Not since he was in diapers.

Chip decided he had nothing to lose. He figured that he might get a free breakfast out of the visit. He was ready for this. He had a fresh haircut. He put on his best dark navy blue suit, shined shoes, white shirt and a red tie. He looked very presidential. He looked good.

He wasn't even sure if this was actually an interview. The letter said they "wanted to get to know you and your interests." What could this mean? What if this was some kind of a dating service? Would the government actually sell confidential testing information to a dating service? There were so many questions and really no answers.

He wasn't even sure who he was looking for. He found an empty booth near the entrance. Almost every booth was empty at 6:55 on a Saturday morning. Except for a group of senior citizens playing cards and a couple of teenagers who looked like they were on their way to hockey practice, the restaurant was completely empty.

At 6:59, he noticed someone sitting in a booth near the restrooms. He decided to walk back there. He would nonchalantly walk past this person and go into the restroom to wash his hands. He would be able to see the person on his way back out of the restroom.

As he approached the restroom, he could see that the person was a man. Perhaps this was Mr. Wright. As he walked by, the man asked, "Chip?" Chip turned to see that the man was clearly not Mr. Wright... it was Chazz.

For a split second, Chip thought to himself, could Chazz be Mr. Wright? The confused look Chazz had on his face expressed that he wasn't expecting to see Chip this morning. Chazz clearly was not Mr. Wright.

As the two stared at each other, they simultaneously asked, "What are you doing here?" Chazz asked under his breath, "Are you Mr. Wright?"

"No, I am here to see Mr. Wright."

"Me too." Chazz said with an uncomfortable smile, but perfectly bleached white teeth.

Do you have any idea what the CSA is?

"My neighbors think CSA was some kind of a Car Sales Association."

"Oh, your "neighbors" think that... your mom or your dad?"

"My dad," Chazz said sheepishly.

At exactly 7:00 AM, a large man in his 50's dressed in coveralls walked by Chip and Chazz and motioned for them to follow him as he walked into the restroom.

The startled friends looked at each other, shrugged and made their way toward the men's room.

While opening the door, Chazz looked back at Chip and said, "If that guy tries anything funny, I am going to punch him in the eye. Do you have my back?"

Chip rolled his eyes and replied, "Sure Chazz. I got your back."

The two friends cautiously followed the intimidating man into the Burger Barn restroom. They were completely unprepared for the life-altering consequences of that decision.

They were unaware of incredible adventures the future held.

Chapter 7

You want us to go *where?*

The Burger Barn men's room had several stalls including a spacious wheel-chair accessible stall.

The man in coveralls opened the door to the large stall and motioned for Chip and Chazz to follow him. Had either of them been alone, they would have declined the offer. They decided that they had come this far and for whatever reason, blindly followed the man into the stall and closed the door behind them.

As soon as the door clicked shut, they could hear the men's room entry door automatically lock. Simultaneously, the restroom stall began to descend like a freight elevator. The descent was rapid. Things happened so fast, they did not have time to be scared. Before they knew it, they found themselves exiting the bathroom stall/elevator into a large room. The cool room had very high ceilings and was filled with over-stuffed leather couches and chairs. The marble floors were covered with comfortable area rugs. There were dozens of video monitors and what appeared to be work stations around the perimeter of the warmly lit room.

Chazz looked at Chip and all he could say was, "That was weird. Did you know this was down here?"

Chip couldn't believe the question and sarcastically asked Chazz, "Do you think all of the Burger Barns have one of these?"

The two turned around to see that the man with whom they rode the elevator had shed his coveralls and was wearing a sharp black suit and sunglasses. It seemed like an awful cliché. Cliché or not, the man had gotten their attention. He seemed even bigger. He looked good. He looked tough.

He extended his large hand toward them, as if to solicit a handshake.

"Welcome gentlemen, my name is Mr. Wright. I am the Regional Director of the CSA; a small agency under the purview of the Department of Homeland Security."

Chip and Chazz stood silent, mouths agape. They both thought that they had been dreaming. This was real. Very real.

Chazz broke the silence and asked, "What does CSA stand for?"His voice was deeper than usual, as if to project some level of maturity and confidence. Chip was somewhat impressed. He couldn't say a thing.

"CSA is the Central Security Agency. It brings the best of the CIA and the NSA under the same jurisdiction." Chazz turned toward Chip with a healthy smile, eyebrows arched, nodding his head as if he understood what they were talking about. He didn't, of course, but he could fake it as well as anyone. No wonder he did so well with girls. He didn't know what purview meant either, but it didn't matter.

"What can we do for you?" Chip asked, his voice noticeably shaking.

"The question should be what can we do for each other? I am going to get right to the point. You two men were flagged by the Department of Homeland Security. The results of your recent talent exam showed a natural inclination for counter-intelligence field work. We have never seen two examinees score so high. As they say, I am going to make you an offer you can't refuse."

Chazz interrupted Mr. Wright and asked, "Do we get one of those suits?"

Chip couldn't believe the question, but deep inside he wondered the same thing and was happy that Chazz was bold enough to ask.

Lesson E

Mr. Wright: "Gentlemen, what I am about to tell you is classified."

Chazz: "Top secret?" (Chazz interrupted. Chip's eyes rolled, again.)

Mr. Wright: "You could say it was top secret. It is very important."

Chazz: "Tell us about the mission."

Mr. Wright: "Mr. Severson, I am trying to tell you about our organization; the mission and other details are for another day."

Chazz: "Sorry. I will try to be quiet and listen."

Chip: "Good luck with that."

Mr. Wright: "Do you gentlemen know each other?" (*It was at that moment that Chip and Chazz realized that Mr. Wright had no idea that the two were friends. Thinking quickly, Chip blurted out, "No, but I feel as if we have known each other forever." Proud of his timely little fib, Chazz looked at Chip with the pride of a father watching his child taking their first steps.*)

Mr. Wright: "Unfortunately, our country has enemies, people who hate our freedom. They are evil people who want to harm us."

Chazz: "Is the threat ~~eminent?~~" *imminent*

Mr. Wright: "Yes, these people want to hurt us now!"

Chazz: "I have to be honest with you, my concern about national security has recently changed ~~360~~ degrees." *180*

Mr. Wright: "So, do you like what you see happening in national security?"

Chazz: "For all ~~intensive~~ purposes, the new plans are working."
intents and

Mr. Wright: "This is important work. There is a lot for you to consider."

Chazz: "~~Irregardless~~ of the danger, I am motivated by that suit."
Regardless

Mr. Wright: "What?" (Now completely confused by Chazz and his remarks)

Chazz: "No, seriously, not to sound weird, but the suit says something."

Lesson E

· Imminent and Eminent-

Imminent- [**im**-uh-nuh nt] –adjective -likely to occur at any moment; impending: The attack is imminent.

Eminent- [**em**-uh-nuh nt] –adjective-

1. High in station or rank; prominent; distinguished: eminent statesmen.

2. Conspicuous, signal, or noteworthy: eminent fairness.

3. Lofty; high: eminent peaks.

· Expression Guide-

360 degrees and 180 degrees- When you turn 360 degrees you've completed a circle and are back where you started. So if you want to describe a position that's diametrically opposed to another, the expression you want is "changed 180 degrees."

· Expression Guide- (Many say it so quickly you can't tell.)

"For all intents and purposes…" Occasionally expressed as "For all intensive purposes" or "for all intense purposes", the proper expression is "For all intents and purposes."

The phrase means "for all practical purposes" and is generally used to compare two non-identical acts or deeds.

Irregardless- once again, the word is "regardless"… AVOID "irregardless"! Unless you are reading the book *Irregardless*. Do not avoid this book!

Spell check will catch this mistake. Saying the word irregardless, however, does not allow for the same type of protection. You must stop YOURSELF!

Lesson F

Mr. Wright:	"You seem obsessed with the suit. Do I understand you?"
Chazz:	"Let me explain. The suit tells me YOU MEAN BUSINESS!"
Mr. Wright:	"Well Charles, we do. We have to."
Chazz:	"It isn't really about the suit. It's what the suit says about you."
Mr. Wright:	"I understand what you are saying. I appreciate your thoughts."
Chip:	"What exactly are you asking us to do?"
Mr. Wright:	"Both of you will need a black light. Do you each have one?"
Chazz:	"I knew that was something I should have ~~boughten.~~" *bought*
Mr. Wright:	"I have a package of written information for your review. The black light will allow you to read it once. Once read, the black light will cause the ink to appear and disappear in a matter of seconds. We would like questions sent to us via a secure email system we have created."
Chazz:	"I just have a couple more questions." Like, will this be our H.Q.? If we need supplies and stuff, do we just go ~~acrosst~~ the street and buy them. *across (no t sound)*
Mr. Wright:	"I don't understand."
Chazz:	"What I really need to know is when do we get an expense account, and access to an ~~ATM machine~~, stuff like that?" *ATM*
Mr. Wright:	"Chazz, you will have everything you need."
Chazz:	"Once we read this stuff, how do we keep you ~~appraised~~ of our questions, you know, our concerns?" *apprised*
Mr. Wright:	"Everything you need to know is described in these documents."
Chazz:	"The pay, benefits, stuff like that?"
Mr. Wright:	"Take a look. The compensation will be beyond your imagination."
Chazz:	"I have quite an imagination, ~~expecially~~ when it comes to money." *especially*
Mr. Wright:	"Chazz, that doesn't exactly surprise me."

38

Lesson F

- **Bought and Boughten**- "Bought", not "boughten," is the past tense of
  "buy." This is also something spell check cannot help when
  it's SPOKEN.

  Perhaps "boughten" is a combination of "bought" and "gotten"-
  irregardless, it's not a word. (Just checking if you are still
  paying attention.)

- Pronunciation Guide–

  Across- [uh-**kraws**, uh-**kros**]

  The word is pronounced without a "t" sound at the end. NO "T"!

- **From the "Department of Redundancy"**

  ATM- stands for "Automatic Teller Machine" (CASH MACHINE)
  "ATM Machine" is effectively saying "Automatic Teller *Machine*
  Machine"

- **Apprised and Appraised**–

  Apprised- verb (used with object), -prised, -pris·ing.
  To give notice to; inform; advise (often followed by "of"): to be
  apprised of the situation.

  Appraised- verb (used with object), -praised, -prais·ing.
  1. To estimate the monetary value of; determine the worth of;
  assess: We had an expert appraise the art before we bought it.
  2. To estimate the nature, quality, importance, etc.: He tried to
  appraise the music of Wilco.

- Pronunciation Guide–

  Especially and Expecially- there is no "X" in the word "Especially."

Chapter 8

Always "Resourceful"

The two "recruits" returned from the subterranean CSA Midwest Headquarters via the Burger Barn restroom stall that delivered them to the hidden fortress.

CSA Regional Director, Mr. Wright suggested that they communicate using the encrypted email system that the CSA had created. Chip and Chazz had a lot to think about; and a lot to learn. That was, if they took the job.

"Chazz, don't you find it ironic that our test scores were *sooooo* similar. Of all of the people taking that exam, our scores were almost identical. Can you believe it?" Chip sneered at Chazz.

"Shocking!" Chazz replied, trying to hide his embarrassment and unable to make eye contact with his friend.

"How do you think that could have happened?" Chip asked in the most condescending tone he could muster.

"We have had a lot of similar experiences?" Chazz offered in the form of a question, hoping to lighten the mood. "I am going to give you three guesses."

"I bet I can answer in one guess."

Chazz lowered his chin to his chest and whispered, "Me too."

"How could you? You are such a CHEATER! Don't you know how important this is to me? I got you through high school; I got you through college. Now this?" Chip tried to be angry with his best friend.

"That is true. You did indeed get me through school… academically. Without me, you would have never talked to a single girl in the past eight years."

"Not true." Chip shot back, trying to think of a single example to disprove the claim.

"Your mom and sister DON'T COUNT!" Chazz reminded him.

Chip thought for a moment and admitted, "Okay, so I guess we need each other."

"Exactly! Look at us. We were meant to work together; we could make a difference. We could be heroes," Chazz said, fired up. "They don't even know we are friends. Your little fib back there was a thing of beauty."

"And how about that? How could they not know we are friends? Does that make you wonder about the effectiveness of the CSA?"

Chazz smiled, "They stink at this intelligence stuff. That is exactly why they need a couple guys like us. Together, we can make a difference. We will change the definition of the word *intelligence*."

"That's what I am afraid of," Chip said under his breath.

"Before we make any silly decisions, let's go back, take a deep breath and review the information they have provided. You have always said that you wanted to serve your country. Why can't this be the way you do it?" Chazz asked.

"Mr. Wright said it was an offer we cannot refuse. What if we don't like what we see?" asked a visibly stressed Chip. "What happens if we refuse?"

Chazz turned toward his friend, put a hand on his shoulder and reassured him. "Chip, we really don't even know what the offer is. Let's look at this stuff and get upset when there is something to get upset about."

Chip and Chazz went straight home to review the materials that Mr. Wright had provided them. They decided that it was probably best to communicate via the email program the CSA Director had provided. Everyone knows that phone calls are easy to tap. Big Brother is always listening.

Subject:	Can you believe this stuff?
Sent by:	Charles Severson (Chazz) On: January 07 2:58 PM
To:	Chip Phillippo
Reply to:	Chazz

What do you think of their offer now?
How about the cool stationary this stuff is printed on?
stationery
Dude, this is the real deal. This is real James Bond kind-of-stuff.
You know that I always considered James Bond my personal idle.
idol
I would hope that the compensation package peaked your interest.
You would have to be crazy to dismiss all the perks. *piqued*

I guess the main question is weather we have the metal to do
something like this.   *whether*   *mettle*

I am dying to know what you are thinking.

Write back as soon as you get this message.

Your Partner,

Agent Charles Severson (I am thinking about going back to
"Charles". Have you ever heard James Bond called Jim?)

Lesson G

• Stationery and Stationary–

"Station**e**ry"- noun- 1. Writing paper. 2. Writing materials, as pens, pencils, paper, and envelopes.

"Station**a**ry"- adjective- 1. Standing still; not moving. 2. Having a fixed position; not movable.

• Idol and Idle–

"Idol"- noun-

1. An image or other material object representing a deity to which religious worship is addressed.
2. Any person or thing regarded with blind admiration/devotion.
"Idle"- adjective- not in use or operation; not kept busy: idle mind.
–verb- to pass time doing nothing.

• Peaked and Peeked and Piqued– (Past tense of…)

"Peak"– adjective- having a peak: a peaked cap.
"Peek"– verb- (used without object) to look or glance quickly.
Peaked can also mean "gaunt and pale from illness and fatigue."
Pronunciation guide [peek-ed]
"Pique"– verb- to arouse an emotion or provoke to action.

• Whether and Weather–

"Whether"– conjunction- used to introduce the first of two or more alternatives. It matters little whether we go or stay.
"Weather"– noun- the state of the atmosphere with respect to wind, temperature, cloudiness, moisture, pressure, etc.

• Metal and Mettle–

"Metal"- noun- an alloy of such elements, as brass or bronze.
"Mettle"- noun- spirit or courage, prepared to do one's best.

Chip also went home and used his black light to read the document Mr. Wright provided. The black light also brought to his attention the potato chip stains on his pants and the arms of the chair where he usually sat.

Sent by:	Chip Phillippo On: January 07 3:28 PM
To:	Chazz
Reply to:	Chip
Subject:	Can you believe this stuff?

The whole disappearing ink thing really freaks me out. As to what I think... I think you should be paying closer attention to the stuff you are writing.

Yes, the compensation package peeked my interest. I think you spelled peeked wrong. The word is "peeked", like a quick look.
(actually, it is "piqued")
I still have some questions for Mr. Wright before I would except this job.
accept
Do you believe that he will have us work together? As we have come to realize, we work well together. Our talents compliment each other very well. *complement*

I also want to make certain that we are stationed somewhere in the United States; maybe even here in Minnesota. I would hate to get sent to some third world country and get caught up in some gorilla warfare political mess.
guerrilla

mettle
And yes, we do have the medal to do something like this. ("Medal", as in medal for bravery.)

See ya later Charles

Lesson H

- Accept and Except-
    "Accept"- verb- 1. to agree or consent to; accede to: to accept a treaty; to accept an apology.
    2. to respond or answer affirmatively to: to accept a job offer.
    "Except"- conjunction- otherwise than; all but...
    Or used as an idiom - except for, if it was not for...

- Complement and Compliment-
    "Compl<u>e</u>ment"- noun - 1. something that completes or makes perfect: A good wine is a complement to a good meal.
    2. either of two parts needed to complete the whole; counterpart.
    "Compl<u>i</u>ment"- noun- an expression of praise or admiration.
    "He paid her a nice compliment."

- Guerrilla and Gorilla-
    "Guerrilla"- noun- A member of a band of irregular soldiers that uses guerrilla warfare, harassing the enemy by surprise raids and sabotage.
    Adjective- pertaining to such fighters or their technique of warfare: guerrilla strongholds; guerrilla tactics.
    "Gorilla"- noun- the largest of the anthropoid apes.

- Mettle and Medal-
    "Mettle"- noun- spirit or courage, prepared to do one's best.
    "Medal"- noun- a flat piece of metal, often a disk or other form, usually bearing an inscription or design, issued to commemorate a person, action, or event, or given as a reward for bravery or merit.

Lesson I

Chazz had seen all he needed to see. This opportunity was a dream come true. Mr. Wright was going help establish their "cover" as International Real Estate Agents.

Chazz would be in charge of sales and Chip would be the financing expert. Chip had been working as a real estate agent, so it wasn't a complete stretch. He had only sold one home, but he understood the language of real estate. Chazz knew sales. This was a natural fit for him.

Subject:	I say we do this!
Sent by:	Charles Severson (On: January 07 4:18 PM)
To:	Chip
Reply to:	Charles/Chazz

I will make this short.

Don't let my plans effect your decision, but I am doing this. Its a no-brainer to me. *affect*   *it's*

Chip, let your conscious be your guide.
            conscience   *(two words) may be*
I will support your decision whatever it might be; but this maybe our one and only chance at greatness, I mean real greatness!

We could play a special roll in the future of the United States. Think about that.   *role*

Always your friend (but I will like you better if you make the right choice),

Chazz

Lesson I

- Affect and Effect- (this one can be very tricky)

    "Affect"- verb- (used with object) 1. To act on; produce an effect or change in: The rain affected the ball game.
    2. To impress the mind or move the feelings of: The decision affected him forever.
    "Effect"- noun- the state of being effective or operative; operation or execution; accomplishment or fulfillment: to bring a plan into effect.
    -verb (used with object) to produce as an effect; bring about; accomplish; make happen.

- Conscience and Conscious-

    "Conscience"- noun- the inner sense of what is right or wrong in one's conduct or motives, impelling one toward right action.
    "Conscious"- adjective- aware of one's own existence/surroundings.
    -noun- the part of the mind comprising psychic material of which the individual is aware.

- May be and Maybe- (one word or two?)*

    "May be"- verb- phrase meaning "might be" or "could be."
    "Maybe"- adverb- perhaps; possibly.

- Role and Roll-

    "Role"- noun- a part or character played by a person.
    "Roll"- verb- to move along a surface by revolving or turning.

Lesson J

Chip spent the afternoon contemplating his future. He knew in his heart that Chazz was right. This was a once-in-a-lifetime opportunity. He had to pursue this.

His concerns suddenly changed from selfishness to concern about whether or not he was qualified to do this job. Was he really right for this job? Was the job really right for him?

Subject: I'm in. What now?
Sent by: Chip Phillippo (On: January 07 7:47 PM)
To: Charles
Reply to: Chip

Okay Chazz, you got me. I'm in.

I have some ~~miner~~ reservations about my ~~personnel~~ ability to do this. Don't you?   *minor*   *personal*

Based on the materials we reviewed, it appears that we could spend as much as 99% of our time doing nothing! Just waiting for something to happen, observing. Do you have the ~~patients~~ for the boredom we might experience?   *patience*

This isn't exactly chasing down bad guys all the time. As the documents described, all the ~~sorted~~ details of sitting and waiting, tired eyes, sleepless nights and ~~soar~~ butts!   *sordid*   *sore*

The lifestyle, the compensation, the potential excitement, the expense accounts and the suits are all winners. I just want to be realistic about this.

Let's meet tomorrow for lunch. We'll finalize our plans. I'm going to bed.

Chip

Lesson J

- Miner and Minor-

  "Miner"- noun- Also called "mineworker"; a person who works in a mine.

  "Minor"- adjective- 1. Lesser, as in size, extent, or importance, or being or noting the lesser of two: a minor share.

  -adjective- 2. Not serious, important, etc.: a minor wound.

  -noun- 3. A person under the legal age of full responsibility.

- Personnel and Personal-

  "Personnel"- noun- a body of persons employed in a place of work.

  "Personal"– adjective- of, pertaining to, or coming as from a particular person; individual; private: a personal opinion.

- Patients and Patience-

  "Patients"- noun- people who are under medical care or treatment.

  "Patience"- noun- an ability or willingness to suppress restlessness or annoyance when confronted with delay: to have patience with a child. Note: "patient"- when an adjective-bearing provocation, annoyance, misfortune, delay, with fortitude and calm and without complaint or anger.

- Sorted and Sordid-

  "Sorted"- past tense of "sort"- verb- to arrange or put in order.

  "Sordid"- adjective- morally ignoble or base; vile.

- Soar and Sore-

  "Soar"- verb- to fly at a great height, without visible movements of the pinions, as a bird.

  "Sore"- adjective- physically painful or sensitive, as a wound or hurt.

Chapter 9

Where the Customer is Always *Wrong*

Chip and Chazz did not even need to discuss where to meet for lunch. Anytime they were looking for a quiet place to meet, the duo went to the Lakeside Club. The restaurant was unique. It had been in business for over 50 years and had not changed the décor since the day it opened and nobody cared. The Lakeside did not have to hide behind expensive furnishings and starched tablecloths. It was all about the food.

The Lakeside was owned and operated by two sisters who constantly feigned crabbiness. To support their crabby shtick, they wore shirts that said, *Lakeside: Where the customer is always WRONG!* In reality, Sue and Cheryl were thoughtful ladies who sincerely cared about their customers. They often made special treats to give away to their regulars after dinner. This practice obviously cut into their dessert "profit margin."

Most importantly, their food is so good it will give a person goose bumps. It certainly made Chip a happy fella.

Chip and Chazz liked to eat at the bar. They had been eating at the bar since high school; it made them feel like grown-ups. It still made them feel like grown-ups.

Today was different. Today they sat in a booth and instead of discussing the mundane details of their largely insignificant day-to-day grind, they had something meaningful to discuss. It was kind of fun, and kind of scary.

"Can you believe this?" Chip blurted out.

"Let's be honest with each other, up until a couple of days ago our lives were nothing but *smoky mirrors.*"

"Charles, um I mean Chazz, I think the phrase that you are looking for is *"smoke and mirrors."* (*It is 'smoke and mirrors', a metaphor for a deceptive, fraudulent or insubstantial explanation or description. The source of the name is based on magicians' illusions, where magicians make objects appear or disappear by extending or retracting mirrors amid a confusing burst of smoke. The expression may have a connotation of cleverness in carrying out such a deception.*)

"Whatever, you know what I mean!" Chazz scolded.

Chip interrupted, "I just want to make sure you do."

"Can we talk like adults here?"

"Sorry, go ahead with your mirrors," Chip said with a grin.

"My whole life, it has been a series of would of, could of, should of…"

Chip interrupted again, "I believe the phrase is would have, could have, should have." (The proper phrase is 'would have, could have, should have…')

"Woulda, coulda, shoulda? Would you zip it for two minutes so I can make my point Dr. Grammar."

"Sorry."

"I am proud of us. Actually, I am expecially proud of you, Chip; and I am grateful." (Chip thought about correcting Chazz again. There is no "x" in "especially." He decided to just ignore the mistake.) Chazz said with the most sincerity of his life, his eyes with just a hint of moisture, "I have always appreciated your help. Your friendship has meant…"

"What do you two clowns want?" Sue, the waitress/cook/bartender hostess/dishwasher interrupted.

"The usual," Chip said, giving his friend the opportunity to compose himself.

"Chippy," as she loved to call him "just about everything on the menu is "the usual" for you," Sue laughed, unconcerned about hurting feelings.

"I'll have a cheeseburger, no fries and can I get a bigger salad with Roquefort dressing," Sue had taught the guys the fancy name for blue (or bleu) cheese dressing.

"Oh Chippy, you do know that the low-carb thing is kind of a waste of time when you eat one of Sue's cookies for dessert, don't you?" Chazz offered in his best "wise-cracker" tone. Sue's cookies were as big as a Frisbee and probably required a shot of insulin to restore glucose levels in even the non-diabetic customers.

"Thank you Captain Fitness." Chip replied.

"I will have the boneless chicken breast and asparagus, please," Chazz politely said, winking at Chip.

"Seriously?" Chip asked, not really surprised.

Smacking himself in the stomach with an open hand, Chazz replied, "Abs baby… Abs. Nothing tastes as good as these abs."

"Feel." Chip offered.

"Feel?" Chazz replied, looking confused as he often does.

"Nothing tastes as good as these abs is something you might say at a cannibal convention. Think about it. You need to add the word "feel" to the end of your cute little statement."

Sue asked, "Are you two married yet? You sound eerily like an old married couple."

"Thank you Sue, not yet. That will be all," Chazz shooed her away with his hand, dismissing her with purposeful disrespect and Sue expected nothing less.

"I have taught you ladies well. Another round of drinks?"

"Yes, another round of drinks for the house," Chazz exclaimed, knowing he and Chip were the only ones in the restaurant at that time.

"The 30 guys from the American Legion downstairs will appreciate that." Sue said walking away, discreetly winking at Chip, knowing it would make Chazz squirm just a bit.

Chazz paused, leaned in and whispered, "Is she serious?"

Chip leaned in, as if to whisper and yelled in his face, "NO, SHE'S KIDDING, YOU GOOFBALL!"

Chip and Chazz enjoyed their dinner and a few beverages. They discussed the next steps and the role each would play in their next communications with Mr. Wright.

They decided to tell Mr. Wright the truth about their friendship; not because it was the right thing to do. They decided to come clean because they were concerned that it was some kind of honesty test. As a well-seasoned purveyor of untruths, Chazz had what he called a "sixth sense for fibbery."

They also decided that they should insist that they were a "package deal." They keenly recognized the strength of their partnership and were not afraid to admit that each others' strengths complemented each others' shortcomings. While not afraid to admit his shortcomings, Chazz really hated doing so.

As they understood it, the next 180 days would consist of intense training. Chip quietly read the description for spy training that he got off the internet.

"Spies who work in the field must undergo training in what is known as "field craft." This involves things like weapons training, recognizing when you are being followed (or how to follow someone) and the planting of electronic surveillance and other such things."

"So far it sounds pretty cool," Chazz offered with a silly grin.

"Even then, however, most of the time is spent waiting for something to happen, and those "somethings" are often not very important by themselves. Spies are largely engaged in the business of seeing and interpreting patterns, and to that end, gain training and experience simply by being on the job."

"It still sounds cool."

Chip continued, "Spy training is mostly class work and studies…"

"Hold on!" Chazz interrupted. "Class work? Not so cool."

"Get over it," Chip said, paying the bill.

They thanked Sue and headed toward the door. Chip put his arm on his best friend's shoulder and said, "Your friendship has meant a lot to me, too." Referring back to the rare, but defining moment the two had shared just before they ordered dinner.

Goofballs? Yes. But they were best friends and grateful for each other.

Chapter 10

Dynamic Duo

Chip and Chazz had shared the truth about their friendship with Mr. Wright. He had not known that they were friends when they first met, but had a suspicion after seeing them interact.

Wright said, "You two seemed like an old married couple."

Chip and Chazz replied simultaneously, "We've heard that."

The stoic Mr. Wright laughed, showing for the first time that he had a sense of humor. "See, you fellas are even talking like each other. Soon you will be completing each others' sentences; start looking like each other," Wright was on a roll and really getting a kick out of himself.

The "dynamic duo," the clichéd name Chazz had appointed themselves, had completed their six months of training and performed quite well.

The training took place at a variety of places throughout the Twin Cities of Minneapolis and St. Paul. The natural seasonal changes of Minnesota provided the perfect setting for a wide variety of training opportunities.

They spent two weeks in early March in Wilmington, North Carolina under the pretense of a spring break getaway. This trip gave them the opportunity to visit with a handful of military colleagues. The CSA did some intelligence sharing with a unique, highly trained military organization known as Joint Special Operations Command. JSOC boasted some of the best and brightest in all of the United States Armed Services.

The trip also gave them the opportunity to meet their newly appointed Field Supervisor retired Army Colonel Roger Neetenbeek.

The six months of training went by quickly. The dynamic duo were excited about the way things were going. Fun times were on the horizon for these two ambitious new agents. At least, that is what they hoped.

Chapter 11

An Original

Colonel Roger Neetenbeek, retired United States Army is a rare bird. A "full bird," though he would never remind you. Like many achieving his level of career success, Neetenbeek was known simply as "Colonel." One might think his first name was actually "Colonel."

Colonel served the United States for over 30 years, from the final days of Vietnam, where he was a Second Lieutenant. He was a Captain in the 82nd Airborne and participated in Operation Just Cause, the military incursion into Panama in December of 1989. He was recruited to Joint Special Operations Command, which is a component command of the United States Special Operations Command (USSOCOM) and is charged to study special operations requirements and techniques to ensure interoperability and develop Joint Special Operations Tactics.

In 1990, he was involved in Operation Desert Storm. In 1996, he served in Bosnia as a Lieutenant Colonel. Colonel Neetenbeek doesn't talk about where he was and what he did. The Colonel is only interested in looking forward. He told people, "If the Good Lord wanted us looking back all the time, he would have planted eyes in the backs of our heads."

Colonel was one-of-a-kind and he cultivated his uniqueness. His favorite quote was, "History is a gallery of pictures in which there are few originals and many copies." Colonel Neetenbeek was one of the originals.

Chip and Chazz were introduced to Colonel during their March visit to Wilmington. After spending years living in and around Ft. Bragg in Fayetteville, North Carolina, he and his family fell in love with the beaches of Wilmington during weekend outings when Colonel was not deployed.

After the terrorist attacks on New York and Washington, D.C. in 2001, Colonel knew that he needed to serve his country for the rest of his life. His choices were abundant.

Colonel was drawn to the potential of the Central Security Agency. He was also motivated by the fact that modern technology provided him with the opportunity to work remotely. He could provide leadership to his agents no matter where he was in the world, no matter where his agents were.

He and his family chose Wilmington to make their home, right at the confluence of the Cape Fear River and the Inner Coastal Waterway. It was a slice of heaven. His family loved it there. After all the sacrifices they had made during his military career, he owed them the gift of stability.

To say that the Colonel was "straight-laced" would qualify as a significant understatement. He did not drink. He did not smoke. He did not swear... ever. His only vice was that he chewed on a cigar. This singular flaw was one that he acquired while serving in Bosnia.

He was in the physical condition of an Army Ranger in his early 20's. He went to church every Sunday, he never watched television. He didn't have time for such silliness.

Chip and Chazz liked the fact that their boss was over 1000 miles away. They didn't like the fact that military technology ensured that their boss was watching them. Watching them constantly.

The leash was exceedingly short for the new agents, especially as the leash applied to Chazz.

During their first visit, Chip connected with Neetenbeek in a very positive way. He liked Chip's selfless attitude. He found Chip intelligent and self-confident without being a pain in the rump.

Things did not go as well for Chazz. Colonel wondered how these two guys could have exam scores so similar. The guys seemed so different.

Chazz made a terrible first impression. Colonel was clearly not interested in talking about his military career. He was only concerned about the future, the next mission. Chazz wanted to discuss the details of Colonel's deployments. There would be no such discussion.

They decided to communicate electronically as often as possible. Neetenbeek would direct them from his home office. The work of an intelligence officer had certainly changed over the years.

The Colonel might best be described as a "black and white-type-of-guy." He actually dressed in black and white. He wore a flat top haircut, as he had for his entire military career.

When he was working at home, he wore perfectly pressed black pants, shined black wing-tip shoes and a starched white button down oxford cloth shirt. When he had to leave the office, he added a black coat and a charcoal gray tie. Very boring and he liked it that way.

Chip and Chazz were required to check in via email with him at least once each day. They were to do so every day, including weekends. Life would probably be easier if the Colonel worked in an office right next to their work station. 1,000 miles never felt so close.

Colonel Roger Neetenbeek
United States Army 1972-2000 (Retired)
Field Supervisor, Central Security Agency (2002-Present)

Lesson K

Chazz was getting bored. For the past several weeks he had been serving as an intelligence analyst. An intelligence analyst is an agent skilled in understanding and interpreting intelligence reports received from field agents. Chazz wanted to be a field agent and he was going to do whatever he could to be deployed into the field.

Subject:	I have been thinking!
Sent by:	Charles Severson (On: August 14 4:18 PM)
To:	Colonel Neetenbeek
Reply to:	Charles (Chazz)

I have noticed some patterns in the reports I have been reviewing regarding the recent threat made on the Midtown Mall.

The information gathered suggests that the hostel's we have been tracking could be a larger group than we thought. *hostiles*

A witness (a FED EX driver) reported seeing a cash of weapons at a home in Bloomingville, 4 blocks from the Mall. *cache*

You know as well as anyone that it is fare to say that our field resources are stretched thin. *fair*

Let me check into it. I will be very inconspicuous and I promise not to insight any suspicion.
   incite

As they say, I will hide in plane sight.
            plain

Ready to serve,
Charles Severson (Chazz)

Lesson K

• Hostile and Hostel-

"Hostile"- noun- a person or thing that is antagonistic or unfriendly.
(Also an adjective-opposed in feelings or actions)
"Hostel"- noun- often called "youth hostel." An inexpensive
lodging place for young people on bicycle trips, hikes, etc.

• Cache and Cash-

"Cache"- noun- a hiding place, often in the ground, for
ammunition, weapons and treasures.
"Cash"- noun- money in the form of coins or banknotes.

• Fair and Fare-

"Fair"- adjective- free from bias or injustice.
"Fare"- noun- the price of conveyance in a bus, train or airplane.
(Also a verb-to experience good or bad fortune. "He fared well.")

• Incite and Insight-

"Incite"- verb- prompt to action.
"Insight"- noun- the ability to perceive clearly or deeply.

• Plane and Plain-

"Plane"- noun- 1. Flat or level surface. 2. Aeronautic vehicle.
"Plain"- adjective- unobstructed, clear, or open.
(Also an adverb- clearly and simply: "Chazz is just plain silly.")

Chazz was really getting bored. He had been working as an intelligence analyst for several months. He was ready to "crack" from the monotony. He needed to talk to someone, but his partner Chip had been out of work sick for a few days.

Subject: I am about to crack!
Sent by: Charles Severson (Chazz) (On: September 07 3:01 PM)
To: Donald Phillippo (Chip)
Reply to: Charles (Chazz)

Hey Chip,
How are you feeling?

Enough about you. ☺ I need some advise. *advice*

I have always said that I am not apposed to earning my stripes, but I am about to crack. I am losing it! *opposed*

A couple months ago I mentioned that possible terrorist deal in Bloomington. He just ignored me. He keeps saying that it is his job to "rain me in". I am sick of this. Aren't you tired of this?
 rein

I need some action and I need it now. They are never going to give us one of those black suits if we continue to work in this hole under the Burger Barn. I am wandering if you would mention something to the Colonel. He likes you. *wondering*

By the way, have you seen the latest addition of the alumna magazine?   *edition*   *alumni*

There was an article about Preston Gorg. He is quite a nerd, but I have to admit, an impressive one.

Chazz

Lesson L

- Advice and Advise-
    "Advice"- noun- opinion given as to what to do; counsel.
    "Advise"- verb- to give advice to; to provide counsel.

- Apposed and Opposed-
    "Apposed"- verb- to place or put side by side or opposite.
    "Opposed"- verb- to contend with; to resist.

- Rein, Rain and Reign-
    "Rein"- verb- a means of controlling; to guide or control.
    (as noun- strap of leather attached to a horse's bit for control)
    "Rain"- noun – water falling in drops from the atmosphere.
    (as verb- to fall down; to rain down)
    "Reign"- noun- Royal power; dominance; period of rule.
    (as verb-to rule as a sovereign; to prevail)

- Wondering and Wandering-
    "Wondering"- verb- to have a curiosity; sometimes mingled with doubt.
    (as noun- a person, thing or event causing astonishment)
    "Wandering"- verb- roaming aimlessly; rambling.

- Addition and Edition-
    "Addition"- noun- a joining of one thing to another; often
    with numbers.
    "Edition"- noun- a particular issue of a magazine, book or publication.

- Alumni and Alumna- (impress your friends)
    "Alumni"- See below- plural of alumnus & alumnae – plural
    of alumna.
    "Alumna"- noun- a girl or woman who is a graduate of a particular school.
    "Alumnus"- noun- a boy or man who is a graduate of a particular school.

Chip was home recovering from the flu. He had been out of work for almost a week and, frankly, needed the break. He was also feeling the strain of the monotony. He also knew that their time would come. This was part of the job, part of the process.

Subject: I am about to crack!
Sent by: Donald Phillippo (Chip) (On: September 07 4:08 PM)
To: Charles Severson (Chazz)
Reply to: Donald (Chip)

Hi Chazz,
I am feeling a bit better, but my voice is still a little horse. *hoarse*

First of all, I am impressed that you mustard up enough courage to ask Colonel to change things up a bit. *mustered*

poll
If you took a pole of anyone in our line of work, they would feel just as you do. It's normal.

Look at it this way... I would be surprised if any analyst has been placed in the field with less than a year of experience. And that is in the history of the CSA.

lose
You're asking for my advice? I would council you to NOT LOOSE FOCUS.   *counsel*

I need some action too, but I am not going to waist this opportunity because I am impatient.   *waste*

Stay cool. I expect to be back tomorrow.

Chip

Lesson M

• Hoarse and Horse-

"Hoarse"- adjective- having a raucous, husky voice.

"Horse"- noun- a large, solid-hoofed, herbivorous quadruped animal.

• Mustered and Mustard-

"Mustered"- verb (past tense) - to gather, summon, rouse.

"Mustard"- noun- a food condiment from the seed of the mustard plant.

• Poll and Pole-

"Poll"- verb- to take a sampling of the attitudes or opinions of.

"Pole"- noun (most often) - a long, cylindrical piece of wood, metal, etc.

• You're and Your- (SEE LESSON A)

• Lose and Loose-

"Lose"- verb- to fail to keep, preserve, or maintain.

"Loose"- adjective- free from anything that binds or restrains.

• Counsel and Council-

"Counsel"- noun- advice; opinion or instruction given.
(As verb- to give advice to)

"Council"- noun (always a noun)- a body of persons specially designated or selected to act in an advisory, administrative, or legislative capacity.

• Waste and Waist-

"Waste"- verb- to consume, spend, destroy or ruin.

"Waist"- noun (always a noun)- the part of the human body between the ribs and hips.

Chapter 12

A Mission
at Last

Colonel Neetenbeek did not have a lot of time for tomfoolery. And despite the fact that he was easily irritated, he could not be bothered by a young person's ambition to do more, to be relevant.

As much as Chazz had a way of getting on Colonel's nerves, he could not overlook the enthusiasm the young man had for the job. Chazz had asked for a field assignment several months ago and Colonel basically ignored the request. Neetenbeek expected Chazz to pester him relentlessly until he gave in. To his pleasant surprise, Chazz had not asked for a reassignment since. He figured it was time to reward the young man's patience.

The CSA Field Supervisor decided to give Chazz and his cohort Chip the opportunity to gain a morsel of field experience.

CSA analysts in D.C. had discovered a possible leak of top-secret weapons technology to a spy known for dealing secrets to the North Koreans. The connection was remote at best. Thus, CSA placed a very low priority on this particular lead.

Neetenbeek decided to deploy Chazz and Chip into the field to determine the source of the leak. The mission was not exactly a red herring, but one with very low expectations, a good place to start.

He was also realistic about the effectiveness of placing two "green" agents into the field for the first time.

Although Neetenbeek hoped that this deployment would "fly under the radar," he decided to provide the details of the mission in an official memorandum and treat it as such.

Schwietz & Hawkins

OFFICIAL CENTRAL SECURITY AGENCY (CSA) MEMORANDUM
Memorandum # 0907MW205

To:	Agent Donald Phillippo and Agent Charles Severson
From:	Colonel Roger Neetenbeek, Field Supervisor
CC:	Mr. Jack Wright, Regional Director CSA, Midwest
	Mr. Benjamin Riley, Regional Director CSA
	Major General Andrew William Jacoboski, U.S. Army
Date:	September 7
Regarding:	Orders for Field Operations Deployment and Objectives

Field Agents: Agent Severson and Agent Phillippo

Objective: Collecting intelligence through human sources, observation and by other appropriate means. Field Supervisor and field analysis staff are responsible for correlating and evaluating intelligence related to this deployment and provide appropriate dissemination of such intelligence.

Subject: Mr. (or Mrs.) Kris Smith, Naval Defense Contractor Begley Laboratories, Apple Valley, Minnesota.

Agent Cover: Agent Phillippo will gain access to Begley Labs using identification and credentials. Agent Phillippo will make observations from Begley lobby and transmit information to Agent Severson, who will be gathering data from MoCom (or Mobile Command Center) located at exterior of Begley Labs.

On-site agent will use laptop computer (provided) equipped with high definition camera. Agent is to provide visual/photographic identification of Smith for further analysis.

Upon securing photographic identification of Smith, deliver information to Field Supervisor for analysis and further instruction.

Additional information is forthcoming.

Chazz was about to pack things up for the day, when he saw the memorandum from Colonel Neetenbeek regarding the mission.

Subject: Mission!
Sent by: Charles Severson (Chazz) (On: September 07 5:58 PM)
To: Donald Phillippo (Chip)
Reply to: Charles (Chazz)

Chip,
You are not going to believe it! I did it!

I just got an official memo from Neetenbeek. I am being deployed and be prepared to thank me. There is a ~~roll~~ for you. We are being deployed together.   *role*

I guess there has been some ~~elicit~~ activity at a defense contractor in Apple Valley.   *illicit*

Begley Laboratories is a lab that provides weapons research for ~~Navel~~ Intelligence Services (NIS)
Naval

They have ~~least~~ a brand new black Suburban under our names for the mission. *leased*

He made a very specific point that we would be ~~libel~~ for damages to the Suburban. We are supposed to be careful. *liable*

If this ~~don't~~ make you feel better, nothing will.
    doesn't
CALL ME. I am on my way home.

Chazz

Lesson N

- Role and Roll-

    "Role"- noun- a function assumed by someone; the part played.

    "Roll"- verb- to move by turning around or over and over.

    (As a noun-a scroll, a list of names, a small piece of bread)

- Illicit and Elicit-

    "Illicit"- adjective- unlawful or improper.

    "Elicit"- verb- to draw out; evoke. (a response, etc.)

- Naval and Navel-

    "Naval"- adjective- of, or having to do with the Navy.

    "Navel"- noun-a small scar in the abdomen; also known as "belly button."

- Leased and Least-

    "Leased"- verb- to contract with an owner for use of property.

    "Least"- adjective- smallest or slightest in size or degree.

- Liable and Libel-

    "Liable"- adjective- legally bound or responsible; subject to; likely to.

    "Libel"- noun- any written or printed matter tending to injure a person's reputation unjustly.

    (As a verb, "libeled" or "libeling"- to make a libel against someone)

- Doesn't and Don't-

    "Doesn't"- conjunction of "does" and "not" is used with the third person singular- words like he, she, and it.

    "He doesn't want sugar in his coffee."

    "Don't"- conjunction of "do" or "not"; don't, do not, or do is used for other subjects. "Don't give him sugar in his coffee."

Subject:	Mission!
Sent by:	Donald Phillippo (Chip) (On: September 07 6:31 PM)
To:	Charles Severson (Chazz)
Reply to:	Donald (Chip)

Chazz,

I am not going to lie... I don't believe it.

Truth be told, I am very excited. I am WAY overdo for some
excitement. *overdue*

I just wish I could tell my parents. Don't worry; I won't breech my
oath of confidentiality. *breach*

Chazz, you played this just right. You have done some amazing
things, but this might be your greatest feet. *feat*

straight

I am looking forward to this, but let's get one thing strait Agent
Severson, if you drive the car, you are the one liable.

lien

The last thing I want is the CSA garnishing my wages or putting a
lean on my parents' house because you decide to chase someone
and crash the new truck while going mock 10.

mach

When do we actually start?

Chip

Lesson O

- Overdue and Overdo-

    "Overdue"- adjective- past the time for arrival.

    "Overdo"- verb- to do too much; to exaggerate.

- Breach and Breech-

    "Breach"- noun- a failure to observe a promise or a law.

    (As a verb- to make a breach in; act of breaking a promise)

    "Breech"- noun- the buttocks or the part of a gun behind the barrel.

- Feat and Feet-

    "Feat"- noun- a deed of unusual daring or skill.

    "Feet"- noun- plural of foot.

- Straight and Strait-

    "Straight"- adjective- direct; undeviating; honest and sincere.

    "Strait"- noun- narrow waterway connecting two large bodies of water. (As adjective- narrow or strict)

- Lien and Lean-

    "Lien"- noun- a legal claim on another's property as security on a debt.

    "Lean"- adjective- thin, spare, meager.

- Mach and Mock-

    "Mach"- noun- a number indicating the ratio of the speed of an object to the speed of sound in the medium through which the object is moving.

    "Mock"- verb- to ridicule, to mimic.

    (As adjective- sham or imitation; as adverb-falsely or insincerely)

Lesson P

Chazz had spent the night reviewing the materials that he received from Colonel Neetenbeek.

Subject: Here is what I know
Sent by: Charles Severson (Chazz) (On: September 09 7:21 AM)
To: Donald Phillippo (Chip)
Reply to: Charles (Chazz)

Chip,

Here are the details of the mission: Agents Phillippo and Severson will be on sight at Begley Labs September 10.
site

Intelligence analysts assigned to this case believe that there is a soul perpetrator who is stealing top secret weapon technology.   *sole*

It is believed that once the perpetrator steels the information, they pedal the secrets to North Korea.   *steals*
peddle

They do not know if the perpetrator is a man or a woman. They believe the subject is named Kris Smith. The D.C. analysts came into possession of this lead just within the last couple of months. Subject has been on the lamb for years.
lam

Agent Phillippo will make necessary observations from the Begley lobby, which is a large glass enclosed hall as big as a 747 airplane hanger. *hangar*

Agent Severson will receive relevant information in Mobile Communication Center and report to his supervisors.

Colonel Neetenbeek will be coordinating the post information gathering phase of the mission. Neetenbeek will provide follow-up instructions.

Lesson P

- Site and Sight-
    - "Site"- noun- a location or scene.
    - "Sight"- noun- something seen or worth seeing.
    - (As a verb-to observe; to glimpse; to aim at)

- Sole and Soul-
    - "Sole"- adjective- without another; single; one and only.
    - "Soul"- noun- the spiritual part of a person.

- Steal and Steel-
    - "Steal"- verb- to take property dishonestly in a secret way.
    - "Steel"- noun- a hard tough alloy of iron with carbon.

- Peddle, Pedal and Petal-
    - "Peddle"- verb- to go from place to place selling.
    - "Pedal"- noun- a lever operated by foot. (as adjective-of the foot)
    - "Petal" - noun- flower.

- Lam and Lamb-
    - "Lam"- verb- in flight, as from the police.
    - "Lamb"- noun- a young sheep.

- Hangar and Hanger-
    - "Hangar"- noun- a large repair shed or shelter for aircraft.
    - "Hanger"- noun- that on which something is hung.

Chapter 13

Stakeout

Begley Laboratories was located in a very secluded wooded area in Apple Valley, Minnesota. The company was incorporated in 1999. Begley built its business designing, manufacturing and servicing radiation detection devices and gauges, detection instruments for measuring radiation in air, liquid and gases.

In 2004, Begley acquired a small company with promising government contracts to manufacture military technology and equipment. In recent years, Begley has begun operating in the arms industry, buying and selling weapons, munitions and other military items. Products include guns, ammunition, missiles, electronic systems, and more. They also conduct significant research and development.

It is estimated that yearly, over 1.5 trillion dollars are spent on military expenditures worldwide, a good market to be in and largely recession-proof.

There were armed guards posted at the entrance of the Begley parking lot. If the goal of these guards was to be intimidating, mission accomplished. Chip and Chazz easily made their way past the guards with little fanfare. They barely looked at their counterfeit identification cards.

They passed a handful of empty "Visitor Parking" spots and parked among the employee vehicles, hoping to simply blend in.

Chip and Chazz spent a moment reviewing their objectives and finalized plans for communicating with each other during the mission. The CSA agents would communicate using an encrypted email program. This program used a similar algorithm to the one used by the CIA and NSA. The system was deemed fit for the encryption of TOP SECRET information. This stuff was the best that money could buy.

Chip made his way from the Suburban up the walkway toward the entry. The exterior of the building was meticulously landscaped with a perfectly manicured lawn and extensive flower beds.

As he approached the entryway, the large steel and glass door opened automatically. The door opened into a small vestibule with three security personnel equipped with a variety of x-ray equipment and other gauges Chip could not even identify.

He thought to himself, "If Begley is in the business of developing detection equipment, it would only make sense that they would demonstrate their technological sophistication to every visitor." The identification and credentials worked. Chip was politely welcomed and directed to the lobby.

Entering the lobby reminded him of the scene from the Wizard of Oz when Dorothy opened the door of her home into the colorful, wonderful world of Oz. The Begley lobby was awesome, completely enclosed by glass and steel. It must have had a 40-foot ceiling and architecture unlike anything he had ever seen.

The lobby was decorated with large, contemporary leather couches and lots of them.

There were about a dozen "techie-looking" employees lingering around the lobby plus two receptionists stationed at the large front desk.

Chip found a comfortable place to set up shop. He pulled out his laptop, powered up and prepared an update for Chazz.

Lesson Q

Chip took a moment to gather his thoughts. His nerves combined with the opulence of Begley Labs caught him off guard.

Subject: I'm in
Sent by: Donald Phillippo (Chip) (On: September 10 8:05 AM)
To: Charles Severson (Chazz)
Reply to: Donald (Chip)

Now that I have had a chance to orientate myself, I am checking in:
orient

I have made it (through) security. The ID and credentials did not raise any red flags.   *(or thru... both work)*

Chazz, you would love it here. This place is teaming with nerds. And I mean BIG NERDS! It's a virtual nerd festival. *teeming*

vial   beaker

I even see a guy in a lab coat carrying around a vile; a beeker. It seems so cliché.

This is a nine storey building. Eight are below ground. Very cool.
story (both work)

As we discussed, you need to call the number provided and ask floor security personnel to send Kris Smith up to get a package that has been delivered. The building is a fortress. While it accepts incoming calls, all calls are monitored. There are no outgoing calls, cell phone signals are scrambled and only a handful of employees with access to outgoing email, those with the highest security clearance.

We expect the subject (Kris Smith) to answer the call. It should take the subject between 4 and 7 minutes to make the assent.

(ascent)

I will wait for subject to come to front desk, ask for package and look confused because there is no package. I will take a picture of subject and deliver to Colonel for further analysis.

Lesson Q

- Orient and Orientate (both work)-
    "Orient"- verb- to adjust oneself to a particular situation. (Preferred)
    (As a noun- the Far East or East Asia)
    "Orientate"- verb- to orient.

- Through and Thru (both work)-
    "Through"- preposition- in one side and out the other. (Preferred)
    "Thru"- preposition- colloquial (informal) spelling of "through,"
        which is not acceptable in academic writing.

- Teeming and Teaming-
    "Teeming"- verb- swarming.
    "Teaming"- verb- joining together to work.

- Vial and Vile-
    "Vial"- noun- a small bottle for liquids.
    "Vile"- adjective- morally evil; repulsive; disgusting.

- Beaker and Beeker-
    "Beaker"- noun- a glass or metal container with a beak-like spout.
    "Beeker"- not a word.

- Storey and Story (both work)-
    "Storey"- noun- both work.
    "Story"- noun- both work.

- Ascent and Assent-
    "Ascent"- noun- an upward slope.
    "Assent"- verb- to express acceptance; agree.

Lesson R

Chazz was outside Begley Labs monitoring the reports coming from Chip relaying information to Colonel Neetenbeek and Mr. Wright and supporting Chip according to his directions. Chazz was able to tap into the Begley phone system and generate a call to the internal switchboard operator.

Subject: You're in. The call has been made at 8:34 AM
Sent by: Charles Severson (Chazz) (On: September 10 8:35 AM)
To: Donald Phillippo (Chip)
Reply to: Charles (Chazz)

I spoke to the operator on Kris Smith's floor and told them that a package from ~~John~~ Hopkins University had been delivered to the lobby.   *Johns*

You simply need to ~~canvas~~ those approaching the lobby front desk and take pictures of them.   *canvass*

Hopefully only one employee will approach the desk, looking confused or frustrated in the next 10-15 minutes. We'll have our guy... or gal.

rite
Sitting out here on a stakeout feels like a professional right of passage. I feel as if I should have a box of donuts and a cold coffee.

I love it. Hopefully next time I get to go undercover. I am sure you would like the donuts. ☺ .

By the way, I have moved the truck. We were parked way too close to the cars on either side of us. I didn't want any door dings.

aisles
I have moved the truck two isles closer to the exit. Don't worry, I did not dessert you good buddy.

desert

Lesson R

The name of the institution is Johns Hopkins University (Johns with an "s").

- Canvass and Canvas-

    "Canvass"- verb- to examine places or groups of people, often soliciting opinions or votes.

    "Canvas"- noun- a course, dense cloth made of hemp or cotton used for tents and sails. Also, "an oil painting on canvas."

- Rite and Right and Write-

    "Rite"- verb-a significant solemn act.

    (As "Rite of passage"- a significant event, ceremony in a person's life)

    "Right"- adjective- upright; virtuous or correct.

    - noun- what is just; a power or privilege belonging to one by law, also the opposite of left (the right side).

    "Write"- verb- to form (letters, words, etc.) on a surface, as with a pen.

- Aisle and Isle-

    "Aisle"- noun- a passageway, as between rows of cars in a parking lot

    "Isle"- noun- an island, especially a small island.

- Desert and Dessert-

    "Desert"- verb- to abandon, to leave without permission (i.e. a military post) with no intent to return.

    - noun- a dry barren sandy region; also an uninhabited region.

    - noun- deserved reward of punishment; his just deserts.

    "Dessert"- noun- the final course of a meal, typically cake, pie, etc.

Lesson S

Chip was patiently waiting in the Begley lobby waiting to see who responded to the phone call.

Subject: Waiting for Smith.
Sent by: Donald Phillippo (Chip) (On: September 10 8:41 AM)
To: Charles Severson (Chazz)
Reply to: Donald (Chip)

A man in his mid- forties has arrived at the front desk within two minutes of the phone call made by Chazz. If he road the elevator just a few floors, this could be our guy.   *rode*

Depending on the floor the subject is coming from, the arrival time could very by 5-7 minutes.
    vary

                          gait
The guy has a very unusual gate (Chazz that is another word for how the guy walks). He looks crabby. I bet he always looks crabby.

        really   *pale*
This guy looks real sick, extremely pail skin, very thin. I am sending pictures of him to you right now.

Chip waited to see if anyone else approached the front desk. To his pleasant surprise, 20 minutes passed and no one arrived. Chip whispered to himself, "Mr. Smith, we appear to have our guy."

Just as Chip was packing up his equipment, he noticed a frustrated looking woman at the front desk. She was there for just a moment, shook her head, looked around and returned to the elevator. At the last second, Chip managed to snap a picture of her, but only the back of her head. What now?

Lesson S

- Rode and Road-
    "Rode"- verb- past tense of ride.

    "Road"- noun- a way made for traveling; a highway; a course.

- Vary and Very-
    "Vary"- verb- to change or alter; to make different from one another.

    "Very"- adjective- complete; absolute or being just what is needed.

    (As an adverb- extremely or truly; really)

- Gait and Gate-
    "Gait"- noun- manner of walking or running.

    "Gate"- noun- a movable structure controlling passage through an opening in a fence or wall or the number of paid admissions to an event.

- Really and Real- (a "tricky" difference... very common mistake)
    "Really"- adverb- in reality; truly.

    (As an interjection- indeed!)

    "Real"- adjective- existing as or in fact; actual or true.

    (As an adverb- colloquial (informal/slang) for really)

    Remember:

    Real is an adjective. It modifies only nouns or pronouns.

    Really is an adverb. It modifies verbs, adjectives, or other adverbs.

- Pale and Pail-
    "Pale"- adjective- of a whitish or colorless complexion.

    (As a noun- a pointed stake used in fences; a boundary or restriction)

    "Pail"- noun- a container, usually with a handle for holding liquids.

Chapter 14

Everything will be fine?

.

The mission was a success… sort of. Chip and Chazz got in and out Begley Labs without being detected. They were able to secure a very good photograph of a male in his mid-forties.

Chip failed to mention to Chazz that a young woman arrived at the front desk just as he was leaving. He did not want to diminish the perceived success of the mission. Admitting that he missed the photograph was an admission of failure. Not admitting it could be career suicide. It could also have significant national security implications. This was all too real.

For the first time, Chip recognized the critical importance of the work he was doing. This was real. A mistake could be disastrous. The stress set in. Chip quickly decided that he would wait to see if the male subject was Kris Smith. He would hope it was. If he weren't Mr. Smith, then Chip had some decisions to make.

Colonel Neetenbeek quickly processed the photograph Chip took of the sick-looking man. He ran the photograph through the most sophisticated facial recognition software. There were no matches. For security purposes, Begley Labs had no employee directory.

Neetenbeek decided that Chip and Chazz would return to Begley Labs the next afternoon and conduct some old-fashioned surveillance. They would wait outside the building, look for the subject and simply follow him home. They would cross reference his home address with county tax records and Department of Motor Vehicle records to ensure that the names matched up.

Chip accepted the new assignment and hoped that the results would help clear his conscience. If the guy were Kris Smith, everything would be fine. A very BIG "if."

Chazz wanted to celebrate the success of their first mission. He could not have felt better. Chip, on the other hand, could not have felt worse.

Chazz knew something was wrong with Chip and asked him, "Everything okay?"

He hesitated and responded without making eye contact, "Oh, sure. Everything is great. Mission accomplished."

There wasn't much Chazz was really good at. The exception to this general rule was his ability to read body language. He had developed a sixth sense for detecting dishonesty. He had been delivering his own fibs for years; he clearly knew when they were being delivered in his direction.

Chazz did not want to push Chip too hard, but it was clear that something was not right.

"Do you have any interest in catching a burger at the Lakeside? You know, to debrief... we can expense it," Chazz offered, with his eyebrows raised and a smarmy grin.

"Not tonight. I am still feeling a bit under the weather. Let's celebrate tomorrow, after we are certain we have our guy," Chip said, trying to feign enthusiasm. Chazz knew better.

They drove home in silence.

Chazz pulled up in front of Chip's house and asked, "Chip, when are you going to let me in on your little secret?" Chip didn't respond.

Chapter 15

A Fresh Haircut and a Manicure

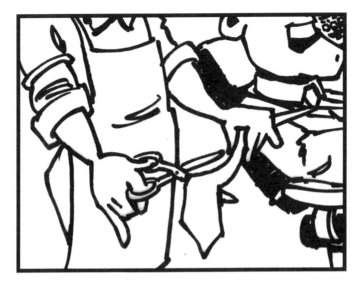

One of the benefits of being a "field agent" was the schedule flexibility that the job offered.

When you had to be on, you had to be on until the job was done. If you didn't have to be on location until mid-afternoon, your morning was yours. You could sleep in. You could run errands. You could do whatever you wanted to do.

Under normal circumstances, Chip could sleep in until noon, but today. Chip could barely sleep at all. He had the most restless night of sleep of his entire life.

He wasn't tired, however. He was anxious. He was dressed and ready to go by 9:00 A.M. He was ready to confirm that the subject they had identified at Begley Labs was Mr. Kristopher Smith. Chip wasn't exactly confident, but he was hopeful.

Chazz picked up Chip a little after 2:00. They were supposed to be in the Begley parking lot no later than 2:30. Chazz decided to take full advantage of his morning of freedom. When he picked up Chip, Chazz was sporting a fresh haircut and was wearing the shiny orange glow from a trip to the spray tan salon. No one should be that tan.

His trip to the salon caused the two agents to be potentially late to their assignment. Tardiness was a way of life for Chazz, for Chip tardiness was unacceptable, especially today.

Chip shared his displeasure with Chazz.

Chazz said, "What are you worried about? You know that those guys don't get out of work until 5:30 or 6:00 and those are the slackers."

Chip and Chazz arrived at Begley Labs at 2:34 P.M. Still unacceptable to Chip, but he decided to forget about it and move on.

They got through security without any issues and pulled into a visitor parking spot that would provide them an unobstructed view of the building's only entrance.

They were getting their things organized when Chip noticed that the first person to exit the building was their guy.

Chip simply looked at Chazz shaking his head in disgust, "5:30 or 6:00, huh?"

Chazz could not respond.

"Let's see if you can do this without screwing up," Chip suggested with anger oozing from every word.

They watched the subject climb into a brand new black Range Rover. Chazz looked at Chip with eyebrows raised, nodded his head and simply said, "NICE."

Chip would not respond. He was livid.

"Pay attention to your job, orange man," Chip snapped.
They followed the Range Rover out of the parking lot. He drove right across the street into the parking lot of a nondescript office complex that had a small sign that said: Midwest Nuclear Medicine "Nucular Medicine? What do you suppose that means?" Chazz said turning toward Chip.

"What did you just say?"

"Nucular Med…"

Chip interrupted him, "Chazz, the word is pronounced NEW-CLEAR not NEW-CUE-LUR."

"What is with you guys?" Chazz said to Chip.

"You guys? Have you heard this before? Please don't tell me that the Colonel had to correct you."

"No, Preston Gorg and his girlfriend were making fun of me and my pronunciation of words. What difference does it make?"

"It just does. Let's discuss this later." Chip said with his eyebrows arched and continuing to shake his head in disgust. He had already taken out his laptop to research Midwest Nuclear Medicine.

"It says here that Midwest Nuclear Medicine Specialists use safe, painless and cost-effective techniques to image the body and treat disease. The company was started by the world-renowned Dr. Josh Smyth, Dr. Graham Connelly-Waldoch and Dr. Dylan Hershey in 1981 and sold to Begley Laboratories in 2008," Chip said, almost expecting that Begley would be involved. "Either the guy is sick and being treated for some illness or he is simply working."

Just as Chip was looking into Smyth and Waldoch, their guy emerged from the office building. He jumped back into his Range Rover and drove off.

In his haste, Chazz turned the ignition key, forgetting that the vehicle was already running. This caused a startling noise that made both agents jump out of their seats.

Chazz quickly put the car into drive and followed him north for about 20 minutes. They followed their subject down a beautifully tree lined parkway right into the entrance of… *a gated community*; with security guards and everything.

Placing his face into his hands, Chip said, "You gotta be kidding me? A gated community? This just keeps getting better."

"Don't worry, I got this," Chazz replied, seemingly unconcerned.

Chazz pulled right up to the guard house and simply waved to the security guard like he belonged there. The guard waved back and waved them through. Chazz never even stopped.

Chip didn't say a word. He wasn't sure Chazz even realized how cool his little maneuver really was. Maybe lying was a sixth sense.

His excitement was quickly replaced with nervousness. The black vehicle turned into the driveway of a huge, stunning home that looked more like a small hotel. Chip wrote down the address as they drove by.

Chip entered the address into their reverse directory link and the name came up; the home belonged to Patrick and Gina Fabiani. Chazz reached over and clicked on an icon that instantly produced a Department of Motor Vehicle photograph of Mr. Fabiani. It was him. Their guy was Dr. Patrick Fabiani, M.D., Ph.D. Smart guy and obviously a rich guy.

Upon doing some additional research, they discovered that he was a radiologist who sold his business to Begley Labs, of course.

Chazz said, "Who is going to call Colonel Neetenbeek? This is not our guy." Chip was feeling sick again.

Chapter 16

Six Stories Under

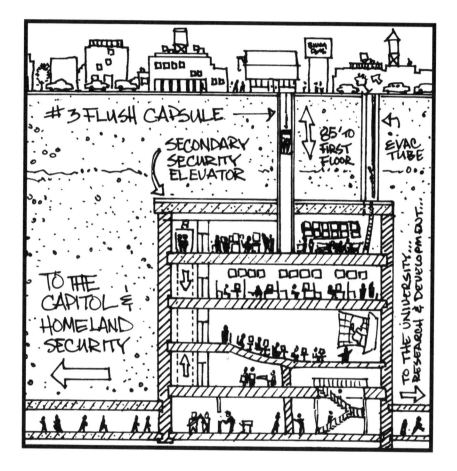

The disappointed agents informed Colonel Neetenbeek of their discovery. Neetenbeek did some additional research into Dr. Fabiani and learned that Fabiani actually had a very high security clearance and did some consulting work for the CSA. Mr. Wright has actually had dinner with the guy. Wright did not recognize him from the photographs. Fabiani had been undergoing treatments for radiation poisoning. He was sick, but expected to make a full recovery.

Neither Chip nor Chazz thought it made sense to press for furthering the investigation. They seemed content with the fact that they would be returning to the bunker; back to reality six stories under Burger Barn.

Colonel had become increasingly impressed with the instincts the young men were showing. They seemed to have a natural ability in this line of work. He was also pleased with their patience. Chip and Chazz acted patiently, but there was nothing patient about how they actually felt.

They were disappointed that their stint in the field was over for now, but they were given a taste of the excitement and it exceeded their expectations. They knew that their best course of action was to lay low and let the process work itself out. Their time would come again.

For Chip, his time for additional field work would come sooner than anyone planned, including Colonel Neetenbeek.

Chip was still bothered by the appearance of the young woman in the Begley lobby. He knew that he had to eliminate her as a suspect. If he didn't, his anxiety would cause him untold problems. He had to know.

Chip decided that he would simply wait outside Begley Labs in the parking lot and wait for the woman to exit the building. His process would be similar to the one he and Chazz used tracking Dr. Fabiani.

He inconspicuously secured the credentials needed to get into the parking lot. Chazz never noticed they were gone.

Chip pretended to feel sick again and left the bunker beneath the Burger Barn just after lunch. He claimed it must have been something he ate.

He traveled south to the Apple Valley laboratory and drove past the parking lot guards. They were really more like parking lot attendants. They did not seem to be guarding anything. They looked tough, but that was about it.

He pulled into the same parking space that he and Chazz had used while waiting for Dr. Fabiani. Not too close. Not too far. The spot was perfect.

Chip watched the front door for nearly three hours. At 4:45, his target emerged. Chip was certain it was her. He only saw her for a moment, but her face was seared into his memory. She was even prettier than he remembered. He was so concerned about his possible mistake that he failed to register her attractiveness. He noticed it today. For a fleeting moment, he wondered if she was single.

"Easy does it, Chazz," he whispered to himself, realizing his Chazz-like behavior. "Stay focused."

The petite woman climbed into a perfectly maintained, pearl white vehicle. It was a mid-sized Lexus SUV.

He followed her out of the parking lot and hoped for the best.

Chapter 17

Hyperventilating

Chip followed the young woman from a safe distance. There was no way she could have detected him.

He started feeling the stress. His pulse picked up, his palms were sweating and he was feeling a bit light-headed. He was probably hyperventilating. He had to calm down.

His mind continued to race. It suddenly dawned on him that if she spotted him, his behavior was like that of a stalker. What if she called the police? What if he was pulled over? What would his alibi be? In some respects, he actually was stalking her.

Chip came to the quick and painful conclusion that he had to let someone know what he was up to, just in case. That someone was Chazz.

While he drove, he called Chazz on his personal cell phone. Recently, the majority of their communications had been made on their government-issued cellular phones. They had a government plan with unlimited minutes. They could talk all they wanted.

He was certain Chazz had his personal phone with him. He always did. He had distributed his phone number to dozens of girls, potential dates. "You never know when they might come to their senses," Chazz would often say.

Chip knew that "Big Brother" was listening. When Chazz answered the phone, Chip simply said, "Hey Chazz, will you go outside and call me back on this number with your phone? I have to check something." He hung up and waited.

Chazz knew something "fishy" was going on. Chip never acted like this.

Chazz waited until the coast was clear by watching the closed-circuit television monitors. Once the restroom was vacant, he hit the small switch that caused the restroom door to lock and the "Cleaning in Process" sign to to magically appear on the restroom door.

He made his way outside of his CSA post like he had every day. Once outside, Chazz called Chip back and said, "What are you up to? You're not sick are you?"

By the time Chazz called Chip back, Chip had followed the white Lexus into a parking lot. The parking lot was for a row of 8 brownstone-style condominiums. "I do feel sick. It's not because of the food, though," Chip said with a noticeably anxious tone.

While waiting outside the condos, Chip explained to Chazz what had happened at Begley Labs and the series of developments that followed.

While he spoke with Chazz, he had looked up the address of the condominium and was happy to see that it did not belong to anyone named Kris Smith. He was relieved, but not completely convinced there were no concerns. He just wanted to be sure.

As he continued to explain his plan, she walked out of the home and jumped back into her Lexus. As she drove by him, he crouched down to avoid detection. Chip put his car into drive and followed her.

Chazz suggested that he follow her and try to get a closer look. He offered to act as Chip's "wingman." "If you follow her, communicate to me via email on your mobile phone. I will provide the support you need," Chazz offered.

He followed as she turned into the parking lot of St. John's Church.

Lesson T

Chip became immediately less concerned about the woman's involvement in anything nefarious. She was at church on a Thursday night. Who goes to church on a Thursday night?

Pray

Subject: Prey for me. What am I doing?
Sent by: Donald Phillippo (Chip) (On: September 16 6:01 P.M.)
To: Charles Severson (Chazz)
Reply to: Donald (Chip)

Hey   *base*

Hay Chazz, I am feeling much better about things. If I were to bass things strictly on my instincts, I am in the clear. She's a churchgoer. Hallelujah!

I am going to stay until church is over. I could use a little bit of church. It has been so long that I have been afraid of getting struck by lightening. *lightning*

Thanks for your help.

rigors

I will see you tomorrow at work. The riggers of the job can be extreme, but at the end of the day...it's worth it. Talk to you later.

Your relieved friend,

Chip

P.S. While I am here, I will say a prayer or two for you.

Lesson T

- Pray and Prey-
    "Pray"- verb- to ask for by prayer, as to God.
    "Prey"- noun- an animal hunted for food by another animal; a
    victim. (As a verb- to hunt other animals for food)

- Hey and Hay-
    "Hey"- interjection- an exclamation used to attract attention.
    "Hay"- noun- grass or clover cut and dried for fodder. (For horses)
    (As a verb- to cut or dry grass, etc. for hay)
    (As slang- to go to bed - "to hit the hay")

- Base and Bass-
    "Base"- adjective- to establish; to make base for.
    (As a noun- 1. The part or thing on which something rests.
    2. The most important element of principal ingredient.
    3. Any of the four markers on a baseball field.
    As an adjective- mean or ignoble; menial; poor in quality.
    "Bass"- noun- the range of the lowest male voice; a singer or
    instrument in this range.

- Lightning and Lightening-
    "Lightning"- noun- the flash of light in the sky caused by the
    discharge of atmospheric electricity. "It has been a long time since
    I have been to church. I hope I don't get struck by lightning."
    "Lightening"- verb- to make or become light or bright; to shine or flash.
    (also- to make or become lighter in weight; to make more cheerful)

- Rigors and Riggers-
    "Rigors"- noun- severity or strictness; hardship.
    "Riggers"- noun- someone whose job is to rig a sailboat.
    (also- a bracket supporting an oarlock on a rowboat)

Lesson U

Chip found himself enjoying church more than usual. Perhaps it was because he was starting to recognize his many blessings. Perhaps he was feeling relief for the first time in several days.

He was also interested in getting a closer look at this young lady he was tracking. He felt like his actions were no longer "stalking." She did not have a ring on the "important" finger, which was a good sign. She was at church alone, also a good sign.

Things were looking up. Chip moved up a few rows in the church and sat two rows behind her. That is when things went unbelievably wrong.

Subject: I am in very big trouble.
Sent by: Donald Phillippo (Chip) (On: September 16 6:54 P.M.)
To: Charles Severson (Chazz)
Reply to: Donald (Chip)

Chazz, I am in very very big trouble. I was finally feeling some ~~piece~~ and I ~~herd~~ something that I wish I hadn't.
peace   *heard*

altar

This saintly looking churchgoer was on her way back from the ~~alter~~ and she sat down next to an unassuming older gentleman.

He leaned over and asked her in a whisper if she had the MISSILE. THE MISSILE. I'm so dead.

She looked suspiciously side to side and handed the guy something.

~~At the end of the day,~~ it does not matter whether I should have said something right away or not. I have learned my lesson, but this is SERIOUS! What am I going to do?

Lesson U

- Peace and Piece-

    "Peace"- noun- freedom from war; harmony or serenity.

    "Piece"- noun- a part broken or separated from the whole; any specimen or thing.

    (As a verb-to add pieces to; to join together the pieces of)

    (As slang- to fall apart or lose control; "go to pieces.")

- Heard and Herd-

    "Heard"- verb- to be aware of sounds by the ear; to learn of.

    "Herd"- noun- a number of cattle or other animals feeding or living together; the common people.

- Altar and Alter-

    "Altar"- noun- a table, etc. for sacred purposes in a place of worship.

    "Alter"- verb- to change or make different.

From the department of "verbal crutches" (OPINION- ALERT)

    "At the end of the day" is a phrase that has been used in two consecutive communications.

    When used in verbal communications, it can become overused and off-putting (distracting or annoying) to some people.

    Verbal crutches commonly manifest themselves in the form of single words or sounds that undermine the credibility of a speaker; these include "um," "okay," "uh," "well," "you know," "uh," "like," and others.

    "At the end of the day" has become one example of a potentially distracting verbal crutch. Be aware!

Lesson V

Chip needed to discuss his predicament with Chazz in person.
He did not even wait for him to respond to his email. He drove directly
to his home. They decided that Chip needed to tell Colonel Neetenbeek
immediately. If Colonel did not answer his phone, he needed to send him
an email. Colonel *always* monitored his emails and responded immediately.

Subject:	I have made a grave mistake
Sent by:	Donald Phillippo (Chip) (On: September 16 7:18 P.M.)
To:	Colonel Roger Neetenbeek
Reply to:	Donald (Chip)

Greetings Sir,

I have made a terrible mistake and I need your help. This email may
bring you some pane. For that, I am very sorry.
            pain
I had a very minor reason to believe that we had another
perspective subject at Begley Labs worthy of further investigation.
prospective   *due*
I failed to share the details with you do to a lack of evidence.
            tail
I decided to tale her. I followed her to church and I was ready to
right her off as a suspect, when she was asked by an older
write
gentleman if she had the MISSILE. She handed him the information
she must have placed in the book she handed him.

Please call me as soon as possible.

Chip

P.S. I am sorry.
P.P.S
P.S.S. I accept my punishment or dismissal, but I encourage you to
bring her in. You must!

Lesson V

- Pain and Pane-
    "Pain"- noun- physical or mental suffering caused by injury, anxiety, disease or grief, etc. (As a verb- to cause suffering)
    "Pane"- noun- a sheet of glass in a frame of a window, etc.

- Prospective and Perspective-
    "Prospective"- adjective- expected or likely.
    "Perspective"- noun- the art of picturing objects so as to show relative distance or depth; a specific point of view in understanding things.

- Due, Do and Dew-
    "Due"- due to, caused by.
    (As an adjective- owed or owing as a debt; expected to arrive)
    (As an adverb- exactly; directly (As in "due west"))
    "Do"- verb- to perform; to complete; to have as one's occupation.
    "Dew"- noun- atmospheric moisture condensed in drops on cool surfaces.

- Tail and Tale-
    "Tail"- verb- *slang* for following one stealthily; colloquial-to follow close
    (As noun- the rear end of anything; the reverse side of a coin)
    "Tale"- noun-a story, true or fictitious.

- Write and Right and Rite-
    "Write"- "write off"- *slang* for to drop from consideration.
    "Rite"- verb- a significant solemn act.
    "Right"- adjective- upright; virtuous or correct.

- P.S.S. and P.P.S.-
    Use P.P.S., which stands for: post post scriptum

Lesson W

Colonel Neetenbeek saw the urgent email sent by Chip. He lowered his chin to his chest. He lifted his head and broke into laughter. He had two choices; he could make Chip squirm or let him off the hook easily. He chose to let Chip off the hook, but thought he would have a little fun first. He would pretend to be angry, and then share "the secret."

Subject:	I have made a grave mistake
Sent by:	Colonel Roger Neetenbeek (On: September 16 7:28 P.M.)
To:	Donald Phillippo (Chip)
Reply to:	Colonel Neetenbeek

Mr. Phillippo,
I ~~could~~ care less about your apologies.
couldn't

I am not going to fire you. I am going to reassign you to a post somewhere north of the ~~Artic~~ circle. You can study the stars with a group of ~~astrologers~~ working there.   *Arctic*
       astronomers

Chip, are you sitting down? If you are not sitting down, I would suggest you do. Your concerns are ~~much adieu about nothing~~.
      much ado about nothing

RELAX CHIP! YOU NEED TO GET TO CHURCH MORE OFTEN...
A **MISSILE** IS ACTUALLY A **MISSAL**, ANOTHER NAME FOR A PRAYER BOOK!

No worries, you're a good agent and nice kid. I was just teasing about the transfer. I appreciate your concern. Forget about it. Take tomorrow off. You deserve it!

Colonel Neetenbeek

Lesson W

- "Couldn't care less" or "Could care less"- (Go with "couldn't")
  When one usually states, "I could care less," they usually
  mean "I could not care less." (For example, "I could care less about
  your abs, Chazz.") In order for one to "care less" about a subject,
  they must first care about it somewhat. Saying "I could care less
  about your abs" suggests that there is some degree of care. "I
  couldn't care less about your abs" would mean that one does not
  care at all and thereby, one COULD NOT care less.

- "Arctic"- pronunciation guide- commonly pronounced without first
  "c"; actually pronounced. (ahrk-tik)

- Astronomers and Astrologers-
  "Astronomers"- noun- an expert in astronomy; a scientific
  observer of the celestial bodies.
  "Astrologers"- noun- the study that assumes and attempts to
  interpret the influence of the heavenly bodies on human affairs.

- "Much ado about nothing" is proper- "adieu" is a silly
  mistake... don't make it

- Missal and Missile-
  "Missal"- noun- in Roman Catholic Church, the book containing
  the prayers and rites used by the priest in celebrating Mass over the
  course of the entire year or any book of prayers or devotions.
  "Missile"- noun- object or rocket designed to be launched at a target.

Chapter 18

Arctic - Bound

Chip saw the email from Colonel Neetenbeek come across his phone. He figured that the response from Colonel would be prompt. It was too prompt for Chip's liking.

He had pretty much resigned himself to the fact that his career with CSA was basically over. In the short time he waited for the response, he had even let his mind entertain the possibility that his actions were somehow criminal. He blew it! "If only I would have told the truth," he said to himself.

As he opened the email he held his breath. The beginning of the Colonel's message made Chip sick to his stomach. He read on…
Reassigned to the Arctic? "What will my parents say?" He thought. He read on… "Are you sitting down?" He fell into his chair and read on…

Relax? A missal is a…hymn book? At that moment, Chip felt a happiness he had never felt. It was a happiness he never could have imagined. He felt relief, remorse, reprieve and renewal all at the same instant. His emotions were kicked into overdrive. He noticed himself breathing for the first time in what must have been minutes.

"No worries, you're a good agent and a good kid… take tomorrow off.

You deserve it!"

When Chip read Colonel's last paragraph, tears welled up in his eyes. He had been given a second chance. It was a second chance to do things right.

He promised himself that whenever he had the opportunity, he would pay that forgiveness forward. He had learned a valuable lesson.

He started calling his friend Chazz, as if it was by reflex.

His loyal friend was anxiously waiting for the call and picked up the phone before it rang.

"What's the verdict?" Chazz said, realizing that his choice of words could have been a bit more thoughtful.

"I just forwarded the email to you. It's all good." Chip said with a new-found composure. "Colonel is giving me another chance."

There was silence on the other end of the line. No response at all.

Chip asked, "Chazz, are you there?"

Chazz replied, "Yep, I'm here." His voice was noticeably shaking. It even cracked a bit. "Thank goodness. I was afraid that I was going to end up being partnered with someone like Preston Gorg." Chazz perked up, trying to use humor to mask his emotions.

"Thanks for your help, Chazz."

"You would do the same for me."

"You bet I would. Colonel gave me tomorrow off. Do you want to go out for dinner and discuss our next adventure?" Chip asked.

"I'll meet you at the Lakeside in 15 minutes."

"See you then."

The best friends simultaneously hung up their phones, paused for a moment and realized how important friends are. Not only is it important to have friends, but it is especially important to be a friend.

They were lucky to have each other and they both knew it.

Lesson X

Several months had passed since the Begley Laboratories mission. Chip and Chazz were back working their analyst jobs and they couldn't be happier. Colonel Neetenbeek would occasionally give them a field assignment just to keep them content.

It was just a few days before Christmas. Chip called Chazz with a special request.

"Hey, Chazz, I was wondering if you would ~~borrow~~ *lend* me your black cashmere sweater?"

"Sure. What for? You have a hot date?" Chazz laughed, knowing he didn't.

"I have been thinking about asking that gal from Begley Labs out. You remember, Kris Smith. I have been ~~buying my time~~ *biding my time*. I'm doing it. What do I have to lose?"

"Chip, you don't know anything about this girl." Chazz said with concern.

"Sure I do. She has a job, a nice house, she is a churchgoer, she volunteers at the soup kitchen downtown and she's an ~~anti-war protester~~ *anti-war advocate*…"

"How do you know this stuff about her? You're not following her?"

"Colonel Neetenbeek calls it *surveillance*." Chip said with confidence.

"The District Attorney calls it *stalking*. You have already cashed your ~~chip~~ *chit* in with Neetenbeek. You are pushing your luck," Chazz warned.

"I'll take that under advisement. Thank you for your concern. I am coming to get the sweater. Wish me luck," Chip said with conviction.

Lesson X

- **"Borrow" and "Lend"**- verb-
    Simple rule: Borrow FROM… Lend TO.
    Borrow- "to receive something intending to return it."
    Lend- "to let another use or have something temporarily."

- **"Bide ones time"**- to wait patiently for an opportunity.

- **"Biding my time"**- means that I'm waiting for the most opportune
    moment to do something very specific. (IT'S NOT BUY
    ONE'S TIME)

- **Anti-war protest**-
    "Protest"- An objection; to speak strongly against.
    (an oxymoron)

- **"Cashing a Chit or Cashing a Chip"**-
    Cashing a CHIT- a voucher for something owed.
    Cashing a CHIP- something done at a casino.

Chapter 19

Wing Man

Chip decided that tonight would be the night that he would begin volunteering at the homeless shelter. Chazz decided that tonight would be the night the he would begin being Chip's guardian angel.

He knew that Chip was up to something for which he was not naturally equipped, talking to girls.

After Chip picked up his cashmere sweater, Chazz followed his friend to the St. Joseph's Community Center, a place that provides meals and shelter for homeless adults and low-income people in downtown St. Paul.

Chip was apparently going to pretend to be a person who was interested in working at a homeless shelter and it was looking like Chazz was going to have to do the same. Chip needed a "wing-man" whether he liked it or not.

On the way downtown, Chazz became distracted. It wasn't a girl that caught his eye; it was a car. Chazz knew fancy cars. He loved them. It was a brand new Bentley Continental GT. Silver. Very Sharp. Very expensive. Very rare, especially in Minnesota during the winter.

Like any car enthusiast, Chazz pulled over for a moment just to see who was driving it. It had to be a professional athlete or some kind of famous person.

What he saw next really got his attention. It downright confused him.

A man who appeared to be in his thirties got out of the passenger's side of the Bentley, opened the trunk, pulled out a large, tattered overcoat and what appeared to be a small, black garbage bag.

He slung the coat over his shoulders, buttoned it up, pulled up the collar and started slowly walking in the direction of the homeless shelter. "What is he up to?" Chazz whispered to himself.

Meanwhile, Chip had already made his way through the volunteer entrance of the Community Center and was looking for "that" girl.

He looked around for only a moment when he noticed "that" girl setting tables with utensils and dinnerware. She was naturally pretty. His nerves kicked in.

Chip wondered to himself how he could be assigned to table setting duty. He wanted to meet her by happenstance. This particular desire was exceptionally ironic, based on the fact that he had been planning this "spontaneous" meeting for months.

He began making his way in her direction and suddenly she was gone. She must have been back in the kitchen he thought. He found the volunteer coordinator, introduced himself and asked how he could help.

Chazz watched the man in the tattered coat walk into the courtyard behind the Community Center. Something did not seem right.

He decided to follow the man by foot. Chazz was certain the man did not notice him, so he could get right up close to the guy without being detected. His instincts told him that something important was about to happen. His instincts told him it was going to be something bad. Chazz always trusted his instincts.

Chapter 20

Cheese Side Down

Chip started toward the kitchen. He could not figure out where the young lady had gone. Suddenly, he noticed her tucked back behind a large industrial dishwasher. She was playing with her phone. It looked like she was texting. He also noticed that she had something tucked under her left arm, but he could not tell what it was.

She was leaning against the exit door. Her face was distressed.

Meanwhile, Chazz watched as the man in the overcoat put his left hand to his ear, he craned his chin downward toward his chest as if he were trying to hear something.

There were a handful of other people outside the back door. Several who appeared to be workers, perhaps volunteers. A few appeared to be there because they needed to be. The difference between the two groups of people was quite obvious and that made Chazz feel sad. He moved closer, confident that he would not be recognized.

The man in the shabby overcoat set the small black garbage bag on the ground just outside the back door of the Community Center.

The back door opened. Chazz moved even closer.

Chip watched as the young woman walked outside through the back door. She tossed the bag she once had under her arm over the open and empty garbage cans.

Chip followed close behind and thought, "Where did she learn how to shoot baskets? Yikes!"

Chazz saw something black land at the feet of the man he had been following. He could see it had come through the open door, but the door itself obstructed his view.

He moved even closer, his eyes moving up the door. He couldn't tell if time had slowed down or things were moving faster than ever. His head was spinning.

"Chazz?" He heard a voice say. He was distracted by the man in the coat who was now walking away with the discarded black bag that had just come out the door. It was securely tucked inside his coat.

He looked away and again heard, "Chazz?" This time the voice was different, much more familiar.

Standing to his left, in the frame of the door was Chip. What was standing directly in front of him caught him off guard. Way off guard.

"Hey, what are you doing here?" He said with a most shaky voice. The young woman was bending over to pick up something. She looked like she was in shock. Chazz was desperately trying to remember her name.

Chip was flabbergasted. "You two know each other?" He didn't realize what he had said.

The woman turned around, looked at Chip and asked, "Have we met?"

Chip gurgled something unintelligible. His lips went completely numb.

Suddenly gathering his composure, the quick-thinking Chazz said to Chip, "Thank God I found you here. Neetenbeek called and would like to see us right away."

When the woman turned to look at Chip, Chazz quickly ran his thumb across his throat making a "slashing" sign.

Chip stood confused for a moment. As the woman turned back toward Chazz, Chip's light bulb went on, at least a bit.

Chazz said to the young woman, "Krisi, I never thought I would see you here; how embarrassing for me. My friend Chip and I were sentenced to some community service by this no-nonsense judge." He used air quotation marks with his fingers when describing the judge. "We got busted for pulling some shenanigans on Halloween. Oh, you wouldn't be interested."

The man with the overcoat was long gone.

Chip offered his hand to Krisi, as if to greet her and said, "Hi, I'm Chip."

Her reaction was harsh, recoiling away from Chip as if he had been slathered with the Ebola virus. She forced the bag she was holding, up and under her arm.

The look on Chip's face was as if he had just seen a pizza fall on the ground, cheese side down.

Krisi realized her initial reaction toward Chip was severe and extended her hand toward Chip, "It is so nice to meet you, Chip." It was said in very soft, breathy voice.

The color returned to Chip's face.

"Krisi is our old pal Preston Gorg's girlfriend," Chazz said.

Chip felt sick again. "Actually, it's ex-girlfriend," she said.

Chip forgot if he was feeling sick or feeling happy again. It was an emotional roller-coaster that would cause anyone nausea.

"We broke up earlier this fall," she said.

"What are you doing here? Do you volunteer here or has the NUCLEAR Physicist business gone south and you needed a bite to eat?" He said with perfect pronunciation and a silly look on his face.

She gave him a warm and sincere smile.

"We really have to get back to see our parole officer, Neetenbeek. It was great seeing you," Chazz said.

Chip had no idea what was going on.

"It was good to see you too, Chazz. Say "hi" to Preston if you run into him." The two exchanged an awkward hug.

Afraid of how she might react to another handshake, Chip simply saluted her and said, "Nice to meet you Kris, um, I mean Krisi."

Chip and Chazz turned to walk away. Krisi started back into the building with the bag still planted firmly under her arm.

Just as the door was about to close, Chazz said, "Hey, Krisi!"

She opened the door back up and leaned out, "Yes, Chazz."

"Can I get a picture of three of us together? I will send it to Preston in an email and drive him just a little crazy. Is that too cruel?"

She grinned and said, "Sure. That might be funny."

The three snuggled together. Chazz pulled out his phone. "Everyone say Preston!" He held up the phone with his left hand and snapped a picture.

Capitalizing on the excitement, Chazz said, "Now let's turn to the side like a mug shot and say, "community service," They all turned and laughed.

"That was fun, Krisi. I hope to see you again sometime soon." Chazz waved to her as he and Chip walked away.

As they walked away, Chip asked Chazz, "Please tell me what just happened back there." Did you know that the girl I was stalking... I mean watching... I mean... YOU KNOW WHAT I MEAN... Did you know it was Preston's girlfriend?"

"Not until she opened the back door of the community center."

"Explain to me what is going on please."

"I think your "crush" is a "crook." I think your original instinct was right on the money," Chazz said. "We need to get to work."

The two quickly jumped into the Volvo belonging to Chip's mom and headed toward the Burger Barn on University Avenue.

"What was all the picture taking stuff at the end there?"

Chazz looked at Chip in disbelief. He raised his eyebrows and tilted his head as if to say, "Are you kidding me? Why would I want a picture of her?"

Chip hesitated for a moment and his "light bulb" went on again.

Chazz waited for Chip to catch on and said, "There it is!"

Chip and Chazz made their way into the bunker, logged in and sent an URGENT message to Colonel Neetenbeek and Mr. Wright.

Subject:	Call us crazy...
Sent by:	Chip and Chazz (On: December 20 7:21 P.M.)
To:	Colonel Roger Neetenbeek
CC:	Mr. Wright
Reply to:	Chip and Chazz

Dear Sirs,

Were not sure if our suspicions are rite, but we have some thing you need to check.

Their our reasons to believe that are principle suspect in the Begley Lab case is the perpetuator.

I have cent you some pictures. Their of the women we have taken from too different prospectives.

We believe the threat is eminent. We have pictures of the car in witch the other suspects flea. You will see that the license is as plane as day.

You're going to have to use the face recognition database! It's obvious to me that they are the ones that have breeched are security.

We maybe wrong. We will await you're council. Irregardless, keep us appraised.

AGENTS CHIP AND CHAZZ

Schwietz & Hawkins

Dear Reader,

Now it is your turn to be Sister Scholastica.

Having read the book, can you find the solutions to the problems in the email? There are at least 25 mistakes to locate.

Good luck. Don't look ahead like Chazz would!

_____

_____

_____

_____

_____

_____

_____

_____

_____

_____

_____

_____

_____

_____

_____

_____

_____

_____

_____

_____

_____

_____

_____

Check your work below. How did you do?

Subject:	Call us crazy...
Sent by:	Chip and Chazz (On: December 20 7:21 P.M.)
To:	Colonel Roger Neetenbeek
CC:	Mr. Wright
Reply to:	Chip and Chazz

Dear Sirs,

We're   *right*   *something*
Were not sure if our suspicions are rite, but we have some thing you need to check.

There are   *our principal*
Their our reasons to believe that are principle suspect in the Begley

Lab case is the perpetuator. *perpetrator*

    sent   *They're*   *woman*
I have cent you some pictures. Their of the women we have taken

from too different prospectives. *perspectives*

    two   *imminent*   *which*
We believe the threat is eminent. We have pictures of the car in witch the other suspects flea. You will see that the license is as plane as

day.   *fled*   *plain*

You're going to have to use the face recognition database! It's obvious to me that they are the ones that have breeched are
security.   *breached our*

    may be   *your counsel*
    We maybe wrong. We will await you're council. Irregardless,

keep us appraised.   *Regardless*

    apprised
AGENTS CHIP AND CHAZZ

Lesson Y

Hey reader, you did not look ahead and "pull a Chazz", did you?

Chapter 21

Well Done, Boys

The guys had done all they could. Right or wrong about Krisi Harmon, they had a lot of fun.

Chip and Chazz decided to go see an 8:30 P.M. movie and blow off some steam. A new James Bond movie was out. They decided to watch it to assess its technical merit.

Colonel Neetenbeek got the message and did just as Chazz suggested and ran the pictures through the CSA face recognition database. He also traced the license plate on the Bentley. Chazz just happened to snap a photo of the Bentley, just because it was a Bentley.

When Colonel saw the pictures of his two professional agents mugging for the camera with their suspect, he simply shook his head, though he wasn't surprised.

He really wasn't expecting any breakthroughs.

Three hours after submitting the photographs to Colonel Neetenbeek, at exactly 10:30 P.M., Chip and Chazz emerged from the White Bear Lake Theater into the dark and cold December night.

Parked directly behind their car in the parking lot was a large, black Chevy Suburban with tinted windows.

Chip and Chazz noticed it, but did not pay too much attention to it, until the passenger side window rolled down.

"Agents Phillippo and Severson..."

Chip and Chazz stopped dead in their tracks.

They recognized the voice. They both peeked over their shoulders and saw Mr. Wright sitting in the front passenger seat of the shiny SUV.

The back window lowered and it was Colonel Neetenbeek.

Chip and Chazz were in shock. They were speechless.

"Congratulations guys. You did it. Tonight, you gentlemen may have saved thousands of innocent lives."

"Thirty minutes ago, armed SWAT teams broke into the home of Krisi Harmon and arrested her on over 50 counts of espionage. She was number 8 on our most wanted list. We offered her a deal she couldn't refuse and she sang like a bird."

"She led us directly to the gentlemen you witnessed in the brand new Bentley. Those men were Mr. Jesse Burns and Mr. Andrew Fox, numbers 2 and 3 on our most wanted list. They were believed to be in southern Florida for the past few years. We couldn't find them. What they were doing in Minnesota was anyone's guess, but you got them," Neetenbeek said with a big toothy smile.

These three had been working for the North Koreans while living in Washington D.C. Feeling the heat and about 30 minutes from capture, they fled D.C.

Harmon, whose real name is Patricia Paulson went to grad school and moved to the Midwest under a new name.

"Congratulations, boys." Neetenbeek handed each of the agents a wrapped package with a great big bow. "We'll talk to you tomorrow."

The Suburban pulled away and Chip and Chazz started to laugh.

Chapter 22

Looking Good

The next night Chip and Chazz went to the Lakeside for their customary celebratory dinner.

The owner Sue walked out of the kitchen and found her little buddies sitting at the bar with huge grins on their faces.

All she could say was, "You fellas look like a couple of morticians."

She was referring to the finely tailored, sharp, matching black suits the newly assigned field agents for the CSA were wearing. They made it. They earned their suits and they were as happy as they could possibly be.

Sue asked them if they had slept in the suits.

They looked at each other and grinned... They had slept in them.

"You two are like a couple of schoolgirls. Can I get you each a kiddie cocktail?" Sue said, rolling her eyes and handing them each a bright red drink with a little pink umbrella.

Chip raised his kiddie cocktail with pride and said, "I would like to propose a toast."

Chazz raised his glass and pointed his nose into the air.

"To our next adventure, whatever it might be," Chip said.

The well-dressed friends tapped their glasses together and laughed.

Sue placed her face into her hands and shook her head. Inside, however, she was more than a little bit proud of her boys.

What will their next adventure be? I guess time will tell.

Lesson Z

Irregardless Top 10 "Things to BE"

1. **Be a "NON-Irregardless" person.** Irregardless should be eliminated from your vocabulary. Regardless is a good word. Irrespective is a good word. You should not put them together. Help stop the madness!

2. **BE AWARE** of the fact that words that sound the same can have very different meanings and very different spellings.

3. **BE THOROUGH**, especially when writing important letters, emails, correspondence, etc. It can mean the difference between success and failure.

4. **BE CREATIVE.** For example, if you are not certain how to use an apostrophe in a certain situation or whether a word is the right one, work around it. Get your point across using a different word.

5. **BE SURE** to remember that "spell check" does not catch all of your mistakes.

6. **BE SIMPLE.** Don't try to impress others with big words. It can backfire on you.

7. **BE CONFIDENT.** Everyone makes mistakes. There are probably mistakes in this book. Be confident that you have tried your best.

8. **BE YOU.** There is only one you. Be the best possible version of YOU!

9. **BE HONEST AND TRUTHFUL.** (Chip learned his lesson)

10. **BE A FRIEND.** (In fact, be a GOOD friend)

Index of Common Problems or "Commonyms"… a word the authors created to remind you that these mistakes, while problematic, are common. Do your best.

100 Commonyms from the Department of the Written Word:

Accept and Except (Lesson H)

Addition and Edition (Lesson L)

Advise and Advice (Lesson I)

Affect and Effect (Lesson H)

Aisle and Isle (Lesson R)

Alter and Altar (Lesson U)

Alumni and Alumnae (Lesson L)

Appose and Oppose (Lesson L)

Apprised and Appraised (Lesson F)

Ascent and Assent (Lesson Q)

Bass and Base (Lesson T)

Beaker and Beeker (Lesson Q)

Breach and Breech (Lesson D)

Break and Brake (Lesson L)

Cache and Cash (Lesson K)

Canvas and Canvass (Lesson R)

Compliment/Complement (Lesson H)

Conscious and Conscience (Lesson I)

Council and Counsel (Lesson M)

Desert and Dessert (Lesson R)

Dew and Due and Do (Lesson V)

Don't and Doesn't (Lesson N)

Edition and Addition (Lesson L)

Effect and Affect (Lesson I)

Elicit and Illicit (Lesson N)

Eminent and Imminent (Lesson E)

Except and Accept (Lesson I)

Fare and Fair (Lesson K)

Feet and Feat (Lesson O)

Fiancé and Fiancée (Lesson C)

Foreword and Forward (Foreword)

Gate and Gait (Lesson S)

Gorilla and Guerrilla (Lesson H)

Hangar and Hanger (Lesson P)

Hay and Hey (Lesson T)

Heard and Herd (Lesson U)

Heroine and Heroin (Foreword)

Hoarse and Horse (Lesson M)

Hostel and Hostile (Lesson K)

Idol and Idle (Lesson G)

Imminent and Eminent (Lesson E)

Irregardless (Lesson A and E)

Isle and Aisle (Lesson R)

Lam and Lamb (Lesson P)

Lean and Lien (Lesson O)

Least and Leased (Lesson N)

Liable and Libel (Lesson H)

Lightening and Lightning (Lesson T)

Lose and Loose (Lesson M)

Mach and Mock (Lesson O)

May be and Maybe (Lesson I)

Metal/Mettle/Meddle and Medal
(Lesson G/H)

Miner and Minor (Lesson J)

Missal and Missile (Lesson T)

Mustered and Mustard (Lesson M)

Naval and Navel (Lesson N)

Oppose and Appose (Lesson L)

Overdo and Overdue (Lesson O)

Pail and Pale (Lesson S)

Passed and Past (Lesson B)

Patience and Patients (Lesson J)

Pedal and Peddle (Lesson P)

Personal and Personnel (Lesson J)

Perspective/Prospective (Lesson V)

Piece and Peace (Lesson U)

Pique and Peak and Peek (Lesson G, H)

Plane and Plain (Lesson K)

Poll and Pole (Lesson M)

Prey and Pray (Lesson T)

Principal and Principle (Lesson B)

Proceed and Precede (Lesson H)

Prostate and Prostrate (Lesson D)

Reign and Rain and Rein (Lesson L)

Regimen and Regiment (Lesson D)

Right and Write and Rite (Lesson R)

Rigors and Riggers (Lesson T)

Road and Rode and Rowed (Lesson S)

Role and Roll (Lesson N)

Seen and Saw (tense) (Lesson A)

Site and Sight (Lesson P)

Sore and Soar (Lesson J)

Soul and Sole (Lesson P)

Sordid and Sorted (Lesson J)

Stationary and Stationery (Lesson G)

Steel and Steal (Lesson P)

Storey and Story (Lesson Q)

Strait and Straight (Lesson O)

Tale and Tail (Lesson V)

Teaming and Teeming (Lesson Q)

To, Too and Two (Lesson B)

Their, There and They're (Lesson A)

Threw and Through/Thru (Lesson Q)

Vary and Very (Lesson S)

Vial and Vile (Lesson Q)

Waist and Waste (Lesson M)

Weather and Whether (Lesson G)

Write and Right (Lesson V)

Yore and Your and You're (Lesson A)

Problems from the Department of the Spoken Word:

1. **IRREGARDLESS** (Lesson A & E)
2. 180/**360** Degrees (Lesson E)
3. Across vs. **Acrosst** ("Across" does not have a "t") (Lesson F)
4. "Bide ones time" or "**Buy ones time**" (Lesson X)
5. "Borrow" and "Lend" (Lesson X)
6. "Cashing in a chit" or a "chip" (Lesson X)
7. "I couldn't care less" or "**I could care less**" (Lesson W)
8. "Much a do about nothing" or "**Much adieu about nothing**" (Lesson W)
9. Nuclear vs. "**Nucular**" (Lesson C)
10. Supposedly vs. **Supposably** (Lesson D)
11. "For all intents and purposes" vs. "For all **intensive** purposes" (Lesson E)
12. Orient vs. **Orientate** (Lesson Q)
13. "Statute of limitations" or "**Statue** of limitations" (Lesson D)
14. "Smoke and Mirrors" or **Smoking / Smokey** Mirrors (Chapter 9)
15. Could **of**, would **of**, should **of**...
    Could have, would have, should have (Chapter 9)
16. Astronomy vs. Astrology (Lesson W)
17. Arctic vs. **Artic** (Lesson W)
18. Johns Hopkins University or **John** Hopkins University (Lesson R)
19. Especially and **Expecially** (Lesson F)
20. Realtor and **Relator** (Lesson D)

Department of Oxymoron:
21. Anti-war protesting (Lesson X)

Department of Redundancy:
22. ATM Machine (Lesson F)

Department of Verbal Crutches:
23. "At the end of the day" (Lesson U)

About the Authors:

John Schwietz is an attorney living in Mahtomedi, Minnesota. He owns a fundraising consulting firm.

Patrick Hawkins lives in Blaine, Minnesota and is CEO of Hawkins, Inc. in Minneapolis.

John and Patrick met while attending St. Thomas University in St. Paul, Minnesota.

Steve Harmon is an illustrator and graphic designer living in Mahtomedi, Minnesota.

Coming Soon

IRREGARDLESS...
ain't a word.

Volume ~~Too~~
Two